MEMOIRS
—— *of a* ——
GRUMPA

JAMES E. PENNINGTON

authorHOUSE®

AuthorHouse™
1663 Liberty Drive
Bloomington, IN 47403
www.authorhouse.com
Phone: 1 (800) 839-8640

NIV
Scripture quotations marked NIV are taken from the Holy Bible, New International Version®. NIV®. Copyright © 1973, 1978, 1984 by International Bible Society. Used by permission of Zondervan. All rights reserved. [Biblica]

Published by AuthorHouse   09/13/2017

ISBN: 978-1-5462-0769-6 (sc)
ISBN: 978-1-5462-0770-2 (hc)
ISBN: 978-1-5462-0768-9 (e)

Library of Congress Control Number: 2017913910

Print information available on the last page.

Contents

To my wife, Diane, who was the first to laugh out loud while reading my pieces.

Preface

It has been clear to me for many years that much of life and life's happenings are lost to time and memory. One solution for preserving the important points is to write them down. For many, that means making entries into a simple diary or jotting down other types of personal notes. For me, it meant preparing detailed memoirs.

Writing has been a way of life for me. During my career in medical research, I have written over two hundred scientific articles and edited a leading textbook on respiratory infections. This style of writing, however, is of little help when preparing the type of memoirs included in this book. The first chapter you will read is called "My Weekend with the Grandkids." The intent was to record details from my point of view during a three-day period when I was suddenly, along with my wife, put in charge of a three- and a five-year-old child. Looking back, it is startling to see how rough and amateurish the original draft was. Nevertheless, a family friend and accomplished writer read it and said it was compelling and had good arc. I didn't know what she meant by arc. She did note that, "It could use a bit of editing, of course."

I was encouraged; I found my way to a retired college-level creative writing instructor, and with her guidance, I worked hard to do some serious narrative writing over the next four years. As time passed, I moved away from purely family oriented stories and began to delve into my own life lessons. All the while, I have tried to look on the positive and often amusing side of life. It is a pleasant surprise to find that humor and charm can be found in many of life's happenings. The nineteen stories in this book reflect that theme, and I hope that these memoirs will allow the reader a few smiles and nods of agreement.

Acknowledgments

Thanks to Jane Anne Staw, my writing tutor, who kindly but firmly moved my pen from a scientific, empiric style to a narrative and hopefully more entertaining style.

My Weekend with the Grandkids
or
It Ain't Over till the Little Girl Cries

"You do remember that we agreed to take care of Caden and Emily while Cynthia and Cullen celebrate their tenth wedding anniversary in Napa, don't you?" my wife inquired.

I could tell that this was just a pro forma question and that "no, I don't" would be a problematic answer.

"Of course, Diane," I said, "but remind me when that will be."

"Oh, you know it's next weekend—and it will be for a full three days and nights. I want them to have a really great getaway," she said with excitement in her voice.

Oh boy. I was staring at a big deal, and it was just a week away. I had not been directly involved with childcare—let alone with young children ages five and three—for many years. Did I still have what it takes? What does it take, anyhow?

Diane assured me that as a team we should be able to handle a three- and five-year-old, especially since they go to bed early. "How early?" I asked.

"Oh, I think around seven o'clock," she guessed. This guess turned out to be incorrect.

The other shoe fell the next day when Diane casually mentioned, "You should know that I've been invited to an important baby shower over the weekend that we will be caring for the kids. You're comfortable with that I hope?"

This meant that she would be gone for about three hours midday on Saturday. The stakes were going up. Was I being set up to fail? "I can hire a babysitter if you can't handle it. Would that be better for you?" she continued.

I had no answer to this question.

My daughter and son-in-law had come and gone during the day. Game on. I came home from work on Friday and was greeted by smiles and hugs from Diane and the two kids. The weather was warm, and the water temperature in the pool still allowed for swimming. Of course, swimming was a red-alert condition, needing at least one adult supervisor who would be prohibited from reading the paper, talking on the phone, or doing anything else relaxing in nature. The preference was actually for two adults.

"How would you guys like to play a game?" I asked the kids. "I am going to give you a grade of A, B, C, D, or F based on the quality of your swim strokes and on how long you can stay underwater without breathing."

"That sounds fun, but what is an A?" asked Caden.

It turned out that their Montessori school didn't believe in grading, so they had not been exposed to ranked evaluations. It was amazing how quickly Caden picked up the nuance between grades and being competitive. He compulsively began working to get As. This went on for some time, until my wife said, "Come on in and clean up for dinner."

I had suggested to her earlier that grilling hot dogs and eating outside might be festive, and she had purchased two of the largest and most expensive hot dogs I had ever seen. The dogs cost $6.99 a pound. I grilled the dogs, and we sat and looked at the dogs for a while as they cooled off. But we weren't alone.

The first yellow jacket arrived about one minute after dinner was served. Let there be no mistake about it—in all fair battles between bees, yellow jackets, hornets, wasps, and the like versus man, the former always win. They have too many weapons. Only traps and sprays might swing the odds in man's favor, but then that isn't a fair *mano a mano* battle. As more yellow jackets arrived on the hot dog scene, I lit our bug candle and announced, "There, that should do the trick."

I have heard louder noises just a few times in my life. For example, when the air-raid horn went off in a noon test in my hometown and I was only half a block away from the horn—and sitting in the front row at a Jimi Hendrix concert with speakers at full blast. However, coming in at third place for loud was the scream emanating from the mouth of Emily at the table. Her eyes were round. Her nostrils were round. And her mouth was perfectly round and emitting an unrelenting and fierce scream that literally scared everyone. No one saw the yellow jacket that had stung her on the left hand.

I went to the hardware store the next day and purchased a bee trap, declaring the yellow jackets winner of the battle—but I would win the war.

After bedtime stories were done that evening and Caden was tucked in, he suddenly presented himself outside his room and declared, "I need to go potty."

Since he hadn't gone for two days, this seemed like good news. I got him on the pot and left him alone to do his business. When he called out that he was done, I asked, "Did you do number one or number two?"

"What is number one and number two?" he inquired.

I explained yet another scoring system to Caden that day.

Dawn appeared on day two. This was the day I feared most. The important baby shower would occur midday, and I would be on my own with the kids. Necessity is the mother of invention. I had come up with a plan.

We completed the first activity of the day prior to my wife leaving for the shower. Our little town has a town-sponsored event each year called "The Festival." About three blocks of downtown are blocked off from traffic, and dozens of stalls and booths are set up for people to show off arts, handicraft, wine tasting, and a wide variety of very unhealthy-looking food for purchase. After a breakfast of my special hotcakes, we bundled the kids into their car seats for the short ride to the festival. To prevent fatigue, the kids were strapped into strollers for this outing.

I was never sure whether the kids enjoyed the festival, but at least they got some giveaway items. The first giveaway was a free helium-filled balloon for each kid. The balloons were inscribed with "Golden State Warriors" and were being handed out by what appeared to be a Warrior Girl. My wife confidently declared that she had tied the balloon string to the wrist of each kid. About thirty seconds later, I turned around to see where everyone was and noted that Caden no longer had his balloon. I asked where it was, and he pointed up. I saw nothing. Both kids began to cry.

I think my wife saw him first. While most of the vendors and booth tenders looked like and dressed like suburban people, this guy looked exactly like someone you remember running the hoop toss or roller coaster at a carnival. He had dirty pants, he was wearing a black sleeveless T-shirt, and his hair was black-gray, thin, and greasy. He was being very friendly with my wife as he demonstrated the string-puppet dogs he was selling for fifteen dollars each. He said they were realistic. "Real dogs will take interest," he said°… whatever that meant.

If operated properly, the dog puppets would walk along the street. "Properly" meant painstakingly careful manipulation of a wooden handle with four ultra-thin strings attached. It was my new job to be the puppet master and do all needed repairs and care and handling of the "almost real" dogs. Soon the dogs began having a nap in the bottom rack of the strollers.

At last it was time to wheel the kids back to the car and for me to face the music.

As my wife left for the important shower, she gave me a last chance. "I can still get a sitter over here for you," she offered.

It was a quarter after eleven on Saturday morning, and I was tempted to take her up on it—just for curiosity's sake. Who could she get on such short notice, and how much of the anticipated three-hour hiatus could be covered? Would I be excused or expected to stick around anyway? "It's okay. Go ahead—I have a plan for the day," I assured her.

Chuck E. Cheese's has a reputation as a great place to take kids. I had never been there but knew it to be popular with younger kids for birthday parties and family outings. I guessed it would be similar to the Cheesecake Factory restaurant, which also has the word *cheese* in the name and apparently serves food that appeals to younger people. I had never been to a Cheesecake Factory either, but I jogged by one once, looked inside, and saw a lot of young people (admittedly not really young kids) eating hamburgers, drinking cokes, and having fun. Chuck E. Cheese's seemed like the perfect plan for the kids and me.

I looked up the nearest location and found one in Concord at 161 Willow Pass Road. Concord is about a twenty-minute drive—if you don't get lost. As I drove, I began to see signs indicating that I had now passed beyond Concord and was in the neighboring town of Antioch. I am always amazed at how often I get lost in general, and in the Concord area in particular. I was lost again. I confessed to the kids, and Emily quickly said, "It's okay, Grandpa, I won't tell Grandma."

A few more minutes went by, and I heard her ask her brother in a conspiratorial tone, "This is a really boring day, isn't it?" I did not hear the answer.

"Why don't you use your map, Grandpa?" asked Caden.

I actually forgot that we had a GPS map in the car, so his advice was good. Using that map and after many U-turns, surface road detours, and miscues, we arrived at Chuck E. Cheese's. I parked a fair distance away, and as we walked across the parking lot, Emily announced, "My shoes are slippery."

I looked down and they appeared fine to me. She stopped walking because of the slippery shoes. "Do you want me to carry you to Chuck E. Cheese's?" I asked.

She smiled and opened her arms.

Kids and parents were streaming into the place. The first things I saw were the doorman and the Purell dispenser. A velvet cord was placed across the entrance in the foyer, providing a sense of control. I wasn't sure what the controlling guidelines were, but we waited until clearance. To kill time, we all applied the free Purell liberally. I was favorably impressed that hygiene was important to management at Chuck E. Cheese's.

"Okay guys, your turn," the doorman said.

We entered a cavernous room, crowded with dozens and dozens of arcade-like game machines. The noise from the machines, many of which seemed to have shooting devices, and the happy children was loud. Yes, there was food, but only from a small take-out counter. There also were about twenty vinyl-seated, Formica-topped booths positioned around the periphery of the room. There was no waitress service, however, and not a single booth had anyone sitting and eating. Fortunately, the kids were not hungry.

The whole arcade runs on tokens. Without exception, it is one token per play. One token costs twenty-five cents, with a special price of ten dollars for fifty. I was concerned, however, with how long it would take for us to go through fifty tokens, so I bought eight, and gave each kid four to use as they wished.

When I was a kid, I was scared to death when I became separated from my parents in public spaces. That was not the case with Caden and Emily.

Once in a while I would catch a glimpse of my grandkids darting between aisles. Their modus operandi appeared to be to watch a player until they understood what he or she was doing. Then, depending on the height of the playing knobs, go ahead and try a token. By the way, the height of operating knobs on the machines eliminates about 70 percent of the games from little kids. I think they could increase revenue if they had portable stools placed around the arcade.

After about forty-five minutes, the kids appeared and said they were tired. As we sat, Caden pulled a small paper ticket out of his pocket to show me. "This came out of a machine, Grandpa," he explained.

I looked around and realized that the operation has a ticket system. If you score well on a game, you can be issued a large number of the paper tickets, which spew out of a small slot on the front of the machine. The tickets in turn can be turned in at the redemption desk for prize items. I looked at the redemption schedule and found that one hundred tickets could be redeemed for small plastic dragons or bugs, each having a fair market value of about twenty-five cents. For the big items, such as dolls and play cars, you were looking at between one and two thousand tickets. Caden had in fact accumulated a total of nine tickets by that time. I said, "I suggest the you save all your tickets until you have enough to get something good."

He carefully put the tickets into his pocket. Emily had no tickets and also no more tokens.

We got up from the booth and the kids ran off again. Suddenly I saw Emily standing alone and crying. "What's wrong, Emily?" I asked in my most sympathetic voice.

There was no response, but the little girl was crying. It was over.

As we walked to the exit, I saw a man coughing repeatedly without covering his mouth. He was close to a lot of people. I began rethinking my position on hygiene in Chuck E. Cheese's.

Driving home to reunite the kids with my wife, I congratulated myself on execution of a successful plan and on learning a fair bit about a world I never knew. It took about five minutes after arriving home before I overheard the kids telling my wife that I got lost.

By day three, things began to settle down. My wife simply announced that she no longer had an appetite. I had noticed that she was only picking at her dinners and had given up on the optional meals, such as breakfast and lunch. "How much weight have you lost?" I inquired.

"Three pounds in three days; I've dropped from one hundred and three to one hundred pounds," she replied after checking the scale.

For myself, I began to feel accepted by the kids. This was the result of a new chant that they suddenly began singing in unison when my back was turned, "Bad Grandpa, bad Grandpa°... repeat."

It sounded confrontational, but when I would wheel around and confront them, they would squeal in laughter and run away. I took this as a good sign; I was becoming part of the team.

The big outing of the last day was a visit to Tildon Park and the steam train. Tildon Park is about a twenty-minute drive from our home and is located up in the Berkeley Hills. Located amid the redwoods in a natural setting is a layout of small gauge railroad track and a working steam engine with about twenty small cars attached. Each car seats four, and is open-air. For three dollars per ride, the kids were treated to a slow and beautiful fifteen-minute ride through the woods, complete with frequent blasts of the steam horn. The kids seemed to enjoy the ride, but they refused my offer of a second round. As we strolled back to the car, I spied a tall, muscular-looking African-American man holding a tiny puppy in his hand. The puppy was smaller than his hand and looked cute. I called the kids' and wife's attention to the puppy. The kids didn't comment, but my wife picked up on the vibes and asked, "Will the puppy grow up to be a small dog?"

"Nah, this is a pit bull," he replied.

Later that evening, upon being told that his mother and dad would return in the morning, Caden said, "Awesome."

I agreed.

The following are lessons that I learned this weekend, or probably relearned from many years ago:

Get a life? This is not possible during the care of two young kids. I don't just mean you cannot play golf, ride a bike, or play tennis. I mean you cannot read the newspaper, watch any sporting event, or review e-mail in real time. The post-bedtime hours provide some catch-up time, but by then you are too tired to do anything except sleep.

No. There are questions that will consistently result in an answer no. Do you want to get dressed? Do you want to get undressed? Do you want lunch? Are you done with lunch? Do you want to go potty? And of course the ever reliable, do you want to go to bed?

Girls are from potty, boys are from... *not.* Rumor has it that girls become potty trained sooner and quicker than boys. Judging from observations this weekend, that is accurate. Caden still wears diapers at night. Diane's big fear each night was that Caden would "pee through his diaper and I will need to change the bed." That only happened one out of three nights.

Car seats. This is a holy issue. Under no circumstances can any adult drive any distance without all children firmly fastened into their car seats. Failing this rule would be tantamount to a pregnant woman taking a glass of wine in public. Car seats are made by demons. They are high, and the kids are basically dead weight (so to speak) as you lift them in. Figuring out how to fasten them may require an engineering degree. Even though the seats look the same, beware if you break the strict ownership of "my seat" among the kids.

Eat your Wheaties. Make no mistake about it, this is hard physical work. While you will lose track, try to count how many times you lift them in and out of car seats, up onto their eating stools, on or off the potty, and in or out of the pool. Be aware that the kids get heavier as the day goes on.

Good news. I do have some good news; it is the invention called the iPad. This is your new high-tech babysitter. You will be pleasantly surprised when you get up at such hedonistic times as seven or even seven thirty in the morning to find the kids quietly watching a movie on the iPad. Whatever you do, if you face a weekend with the grandkids, get an iPad.

Telluride

Xanadu, the Lost Ark, the Holy Grail, Telluride.

I have skied for most of my life and have visited most of the well-known ski resorts in the United States, as well as a few in Europe. However, one resort has been elusive, nay mystical. The resort in question is Telluride, Colorado. For me, Telluride had become more of a concept rather than just another ski town. Located far from normal travel routes and associated with many amazing and hard-to-verify stories, I have been intimidated to the point of making no plans ever to visit.

"The next item for the live auction tonight is four nights at a beautiful four-bedroom condominium, located right on the ski slopes of Telluride, Colorado," shouted the auctioneer at the local library charity event.

I had strict orders from my wife not to bid on anything, but what could I do? I felt a rush of excitement, ran down the stairs to the front row of the audience, and with a pounding heart I raised my paddle. From the corner of my eye, I saw my wife staring at me in horror, but I was out of her reach. "Sold to the man with the plaid shirt," purred the auctioneer.

I was the man in the plaid shirt.

"Well, now that we have to do this trip, let's at least make it a family affair," said my wife as we arrived home that evening.

And, so it was.

My wife and I soon realized why many people avoid Telluride as a ski destination. It is one of those places that you can't get there from here. After two separate flights, originating in San Francisco and ending at the Montrose, Colorado, airport, about five hours had elapsed. This portion of the trip was followed by a two-hour van ride, mainly traveling through nondescript farmland. We did have a moment of excitement as we passed Ralph Lauren's Double RL Ranch, where his large herd of cattle roams. The van began to climb as we finally approached Telluride. This remote town is nestled high in the mountains and accessible only by steep and winding roads. The arduous trip was capped off by the inability of our van driver to locate our condominium building. We finally walked into our building for check-in. Nine hours had elapsed, door-to-door.

As advertised, the condominium was large and beautifully furnished. Every piece was designer influenced, and the place was as neat as a pin. "Is this a place for three kids, all under age six?" I asked my wife.

"We will need to hand down some rules and keep an eye on them. I agree, this is not a typical family-style condo," my wife replied in a voice softer than usual.

Kids arrived the next day. First to join the party were daughter, Cynthia, her husband, Cullen, and their two kids, Caden, age five, and Emily, age three. They arrived from Seattle, flying directly into Telluride Airport. At first, I thought maybe I had been mistaken about the remote access to Telluride. After all, it turns out that they have a small airport. I later learned however that only about 15 percent of scheduled flights make it in and out of the airport. I'll stick to remote.

Late that afternoon, my son, James, and his two-year old son, Cole, arrived from San Diego. Our newest grandchild, Beau, had just been born, so mother Stacey and the baby did not make the trip from San Diego. "Boy, I made it just in time," James declared.

"What do you mean?" I asked.

"I mean that this is the first day all week that I haven't vomited," he said cheerfully.

I quickly washed my hands with Purell, as did my wife.

"How about Cole?" I continued.

"Oh, he hasn't vomited for three days," James reassured.

That evening, the kids were herded into a room with bunk beds. None of them had seen or used a bunk bed, and the reaction was varied. Both Caden and Emily argued over who could have the top bunk and were eager to get to bed. Meanwhile, Cole took one look at the situation and screamed with terror. He slept with his father that night.

Dawn appeared with the winter sun and a beautiful clear sky beckoning us for our first ski day. After breakfast, we all dressed for the day with warm ski apparel. Well, almost all of us dressed. Cole had never seen skiwear, and in fact had never seen snow. He simply would not put on the snowsuit. "Okay, let's take him outside and let him see how cold it can be without proper clothes," I declared, with some level of assurance that logic would prevail.

Logic did not prevail. Cole not only insisted on wearing only his usual Southern California outfit, consisting of a tee shirt, shorts, and sandals, he also refused a cap or gloves. After about two minutes, he sat down in the snow and began to cry. No amount of reasoning, cajoling, or even threatening resulted in progress. He also began to cry, "Mommy, Mommy."

We were better organized the next day. My wife had volunteered in advance to stay home with Cole, assuming correctly that he was not going to ski during the trip. This meant that everyone else was free to ski. As a special treat, my son announced, "Dad, it's been a long time since we did a father-son ski day. Let's go for it."

Later, as James and I were nearing the top of the longest ski lift, I felt a twinge of a cramp in my stomach. The twinge grew to a full-fledged ache as I unloaded from the ski lift. We were now so high on the mountain that there were few if any trees. It was a beautiful place with 360-degree views. The air was clear, the sky blue, and I felt horrible. "Let's wait a minute before we start down," I requested.

"What's wrong, Dad?" James replied with a worried expression.

"It's my°..." I tried.

Suddenly, I doubled over and vomited profusely. After a few minutes passed, I vomited again.

"Oh, don't worry about that, sir; it's just the altitude getting to you," declared a male skier standing nearby.

James and I knew better. The Purell hadn't worked.

Suddenly, I began to laugh uncontrollably. "Hey, Dad, this isn't funny. How are we going to get you down?" James stuttered.

I couldn't stop laughing. One reason was that I suddenly felt much better. Another reason was the preposterous scene, with an old man and his son atop a nine-thousand-foot mountain peak, puking his guts out onto the snow in front of numerous stunned skiers. I finally got control of myself and said, "Just call Mom, tell her we're on the way down, and that I am done for the day."

The call was made, and we were assured of a welcome party at mountain base. I assured James that I was capable of skiing. He looked at me skeptically but agreed that we could give it a try. I was proud of myself as I carefully carved my skies down the mountain. And, sure enough, there they were. My wife, Cythnia, Caden, and Emily were waiting with worried looks on their faces. Cole was not there.

"Okay, I am taking your rental skies back," my wife said. "And you get back to the condo and get right into bed."

For the last day of skiing, I was nowhere to be seen. My wife had issued strict orders that I was to be in my room and no one was to come near me. A few furtive peaks in occurred, but the kids had no idea what had happened to Grandpa. I was taken out of mainstream life.

Departure day came, and I was allowed out of my room to say my goodbyes. I was feeling much better and hadn't vomited for twenty-four hours. "You can say goodbye, but do not touch Grandpa," my wife instructed.

Suddenly, Emily streaked across the room, jumped up onto my lap, and gave me a big kiss. She was the only one to kiss me goodbye, and I was very grateful.

After everyone left, I breathed a sigh of relief, and said to my wife, "Well, my GI upset was too bad, but at least we made it through without damaging anything in this beautiful place."

"Come into the TV room, and let me show you the ottoman," she replied.

I had admired the ottoman as a particularly beautifully upholstered piece during the stay. I hoped that she just wanted to share her admiration of this piece of furniture. But, of course, this was more serious.

"I tried to keep magic markers out of the kids' hands during the stay, but Cole was persistent," she noted.

The beautiful ottoman was now festooned with some new decorations. These were swirls and oddly shaped designs, all added to the fabric in the medium of red magic marker. "Oh no, what will we do?" I mumbled.

"I am going down to see the concierge right now and try to arrange for the cleaning service to come quickly," she responded in her best crisis tone of voice.

After a short time, she reappeared and announced that the concierge had been fired. "I obtained the number of the cleaning service and called them. They will be in later in the week and see what they can do with the damaged ottoman," she explained.

"See what they can do," I exclaimed. "Do you mean they may not be able to do anything?"

The rest of the ottoman caper is an example of a perfect storm. About three months later, my wife received an unpleasant call from the head of our local library. The series of events after we left apparently was: the cleaners couldn't locate the ottoman in the living room and left. They never looked in the TV room; the owner showed up about a month after we departed, found the ottoman, and freaked out; she informed the library and said she would never donate her nice place again; the ottoman needed to be sent out for special services. Naturally, the bill was sent to us.

As my memories of the Telluride visit recede with time, the place has once again become a mystical spot never to be visited again.

My Birthday with the Family

"We need a family event to celebrate your seventieth birthday," said my wife in January 2013.

Sure enough, I was to turn seventy years old on March 23. Given that *celebrate* and *turning seventy* didn't seem to be consistent concepts for me, I asked if we could keep it low-key. "Perhaps we can have a conference call, and the family could all sing happy birthday to me. Or perhaps we can try to figure out how to use Skype and connect everyone through cyberspace for a happy moment," I proposed.

"No, we need an off-site get together in a resort setting," my wife insisted

Unbeknownst to me, the decision had already been made; it was just a matter of where and when.

I decided that I had better get onboard with planning before it was too late to have any influence on the event. "How about a family ski trip to Deer Valley in mid-March, around the time of my birthday?" I suggested.

My wife politely informed me, "March is going to be hard for both families because the kids have preschool classes, which have been paid for and are important not to miss."

The earliest time that seemed to be good for everyone was going to be June. So much for a ski trip.

"How about Hawaii?" I asked.

From my wife's reaction, I could tell that I had guessed the plan and that research was already in place.

"Great idea!" my wife exclaimed. "Several of our friends have enjoyed a place called Mauna Lani Point, and I can even show you a picture of the place on the computer."

"Ok," I said. "I think it a bit odd to celebrate my birthday in June, but the location sounds great."

Indeed, planning was well underway. Rather than finding a large house to live in together, each family would have their own condo. My wife had already scoped out two units on the ground floor of the same building for the kids and a separate unit in a different building for us. This would turn out to be an ideal arrangement. As for rental cars, there was a lot of discussion on whether we needed three cars or whether we could share two cars or even one large van. As it turned out, we reserved two cars, plus my wife reserved one large van. I was amused that only twice over the entire trip were more than two people in the large van at one time. And finally, I was promised that I would be able to play golf, at least twice. I did play°… twice.

My wife and I arrived in the early afternoon and picked up our van. I have never driven a van nor worked the doors and trunk. It turns out that there are buttons to automatically close these heavy parts. "Be careful," my wife warned. "Those doors can close on hands or fingers."

We met the kids at the check-in office, received our keys. and received an orientation, complete with a list of phone numbers to call for questions or emergencies. "Remember, after ten p.m. our desk closes, and there are no numbers to call for questions or emergencies," the pleasant lady told us.

In fact, in looking over the list of resort phone numbers later, I noted no number specific for Security.

The layout was perfect. The resort was divided into separate buildings, all fronting a huge lawn, hole fifteen on the golf course, and the ocean.

Each building contained six to nine condo units, and each building was identified by a letter (A through K, I believe). My wife and I were in building C on the second floor. The kids each had a condo unit in building E on the ground floor. They were separated by one unit, so they could easily walk over to visit one another. Importantly, while it was possible to walk on the big lawn from our building to theirs, and vice versa, one could not see building C from building E.

About four in the afternoon, I heard a tap on our door. "Hi, Dad, this looks great," my son said.

We sat together, and after a little small talk, he said, "Dad, what is the plan this week?"

I know him well, and what he was asking was what level of direction, influence, and lack of flexibility was I going to take into the activities for the week. I had already assured my wife prior to the trip that I was going to take a surprisingly (for me) low-key approach to the outing. She was cautiously optimistic.

"I am going to be highly flexible," I committed. "In fact, consider me the caboose on the train this week. I am along for the ride and fun."

"Wow," he said, "the caboose."

He mumbled this several more times and then said he was looking forward to a great time. I gave him a hug, and he left. I had never been a caboose before and wondered what I had meant by that.

That evening, my daughter and son-in-law hosted the family for dinner on the patio of their condo. Shortly after arrival, my wife distributed white baseball caps to everyone with the inscription "Grumpa 3–23–13" on the front.

It was already bright sunlight when I awoke the next morning. I went out on our second-floor patio and scanned the beautiful and tranquil scene. "This is perfect," I said to myself, a safe harbor away from the chaos of the little kids but access to them when I choose. I immediately pledged that mornings would be mine, sitting on the patio drinking coffee and reading the local paper.

"Hey, Dad," someone exclaimed.

At first I couldn't tell who was being called and certainly hoped it wasn't me. Then I saw them. Distant on the horizon of the big lawn was my son, James, along with four-year-old Cole and eighteen-month-old Beau (Bo Bo). They were all walking hand in hand in the direction of Building C. I wondered where they were headed. I didn't answer back and in fact retreated quickly back into the condo. I peeked out the window and didn't see them. Suddenly there was a knock on our door. I opened the door to find my son, Cole, and Beau. Cole and Beau were wearing matching Superman pajamas complete with capes.

Cole had a small squirt bottle of water and proceeded to start a job of cleaning the already spotlessly clean glass walls on our patio. I got that stopped quickly. My son began staring at me and then blurted out, "Dad, you're missing a tooth."

I was in the waiting period for a tooth implant, during which one wears a temporary prosthetic tooth. I had not inserted the tooth yet, and he seemed pretty concerned.

I asked him if he had eaten breakfast, and he said yes. I fixed a single fried egg for myself in a small pan. Suddenly there was another knock on the door. Consistent with the way my plan for a quiet, hermit-like morning was turning out, son-in-law Cullen, his kids, Caden, age four, and Emily, age three, plus my daughter, Cynthia, walked in. "Hey Jim, do you mind if I have an egg?" Cullen asked.

"No problem, Cullen, the pan is still out," I offered.

I noticed him getting out a much larger pan. "Why are you doing that?" I asked.

"Oh, I actually have an order for several eggs," he answered.

Meanwhile, I noticed out the corner of my eye some serious activity on the patio. Caden had taken over the squirt bottle from Cole and had efficiently covered the entirety of glass walls surrounding the patio with streaks of water, which was awaiting his finishing touch of rubbing it down with his hands. Cole was watching like a student studies with his mentor. Beau was also attempting to assist with the rubdown phase. This had turned into a pretty big project.

Later, after all had departed, my wife reminded me that this trip represented an unusual opportunity for me, but she didn't fully explain what that meant. I guess she left it for me to figure out.

That evening my son and daughter-in-law hosted the family dinner at their condo. Immediately after I arrived, it was clear that both Cole and Caden were hyperactive and focused on me. They didn't wait long before bringing out a partially torn empty grocery bag with writing on it. They jointly handed it to me and said, "Happy Birthday, Grandpa."

I noticed they had each printed their name on the bag. Then they started jumping up and down continuously and told me to open it. I noticed that there was a small bulge in the bag. I reached in to find a well-worn golf ball. "They found the ball on the lawn today and wanted to share it with you since you play golf," my daughter-in-law, Stacey, explained.

This was my present, so I put it in my pocket. Suddenly they both attacked me squealing and reaching into my pocket to retrieve the ball. They were aggressive, and I was harassed for several minutes with attempts to pick my pocket. Finally, they gave up.

My wife and I returned to our condo late that night after lots of food, conversation, and adult beverages. I looked at my watch to see that it was 11:30 p.m. I also reached into my pocket to find our key, and it wasn't there. Knowing better, I asked my wife if she had the key. We were locked out. My wife said I should call Security. I didn't know what number that might be, and then I remembered there was no number to call at that time of night.

I called my son's condo, where we had just been, but no answer. Next I called Cullen, who not only answered but said he would be right over. He said, "My key works in James' condo, so maybe it will work in yours."

He arrived in an amazingly short time, and I could tell that he was in high gear. Unfortunately, he had no luck with his key in our door. My wife again suggested calling Security. Suddenly Cullen disappeared. He didn't say goodbye. Just as my wife started to suggest that I call Security, the front door of our condo opened and out popped Cullen. "I scaled the patio side of the building to the second floor and found the sliding glass doors to be unlocked," he panted.

He is about six feet tall and in good condition, but he isn't Spiderman or a Navy Seal (to my knowledge). The next day I asked for details. "I simply went to your patio, put a chair on a table and climbed up on top of the chair," he explained. "This allowed me to reach up and find a ledge to use for a hand hold. I pulled myself up with one arm and finally got over the patio wall."

Later, I took a careful look and found absolutely no ledge on the second floor that he could have used. Furthermore, even at his height of six feet, the table-chair perch would not have allowed him to touch the patio above. This mystery will not be solved. The mystery of our lost key was solved, however. The next day, my son said he found my key on the floor of his condo, most likely having been pulled out of my pocket during my scuffle with the pickpockets.

Finally, the main event was to take place. The all-adult dinner in my honor was to take place at the Four Seasons Hotel beachside restaurant. Two veteran babysitters arrived at 6:00 p.m., each in their midfifties. Young girls do not babysit on the island, I was told, as the money wasn't good enough. For the first time on the trip (Day 4), we actually needed to use the six-seat van my wife had rented.

"Wow, what a beautiful place!" my daughter exclaimed as we approached the Four Seasons Hotel.

We arrived at 7:00 p.m. for our 8:00 p.m. dinner reservation. This early arrival was on purpose, as the group wanted to enjoy cocktails before dinner at the beachside bar. "I'll have a Mai Tai," I piped up to the waiter.

I normally have a glass of wine rather than a cocktail, but tonight was special. Except for my wife, the others followed suit. The waiter brought the Mai Tais and proudly announced, "These are the best on the island."

My daughter took a sip and proclaimed, "That is the strongest Mai Tai I have ever had."

At eight o'clock we promptly presented ourselves to the beautiful hostess for the restaurant. "We are celebrating my dad's birthday. He is turning fifty-six," my son explained to the hostess.

The beautiful hostess pretended to believe that, but I think the computer reservation from my wife said otherwise. The wine list was good, and I was put in charge of that. For a short time, I was not to be the caboose. After some white wine, it was time for red. I called the manager over and asked, "Do you have some red wine that is on the light side and under fourteen percent alcohol?"

He disappeared and within minutes came back with a bottle of red wine tucked under his arm. He said that the owner of a winery was in the restaurant and had provided a bottle of his own wine for this occasion; although, we would have to pay for it. Being a nice person, I didn't want to hurt anyone's feelings, so I agreed that we would buy the bottle. I did say, "Just for fun, could you open it and not show me the label? I want to see if I can guess what it is."

Wine has been a hobby of mine for some time, so this was more than an idle game. I took a taste and said, "I think this is a Southern California pinot noir."

The manager looked surprised and said, "You should take over my job. This wine is a pinot noir from near Santa Barbara. I did fudge a bit on the alcohol; it is 14.7 percent."

The next day, I couldn't recall exactly what was served for my special birthday dessert (a fried banana with ice cream, I was told). I do recall the singing of Happy Birthday, a nice way to end the evening.

Even in paradise, not every day is perfect. I was not in top shape when I arose in the morning but was still able to appreciate the beautiful morning. I noted on my smartphone, however, that the market was already down by two hundred points. Just as my wife arose, I saw the fly. "Damn, I thought I got that fly yesterday," I said.

She looked over and said, "Which one?"

I then noticed that there were probably five to seven flies on the big glass sliding door. My wife opined, "There must have been a hatching."

That sounded a reasonable. I got busy shooing the flies out an open door. They were easy to coax out into the beautiful morning, and before long the first hatching was gone. Two more hatchings were dealt with over the course of the day, but after that, our fly day was over.

Later that morning, as we sat down with the family to plan the day, I noticed that Cullen, James, Cole, and Caden appeared to be packing up to go somewhere. "The boys are going on a long drive to a state park today," my daughter explained.

But it wasn't clear whether Beau was included with the boys. "Oh, and Dad—Stacey, and I have a three-hour spa appointment at ten o'clock this morning," my daughter continued.

Beau had become the eight hundred pound gorilla in the room. There was now a pregnant pause. "Don't worry, Dad and I will watch Bo Bo. You guys just have fun," my wife suddenly offered on our behalf.

After an action-packed morning with Bo Bo at the beach, a tired grandmother and grandfather escorted him back to the condo. A moment of hope for my wife and me arose around noon, when it appeared that Bo Bo was sleepy and may be headed for a nap. We carefully changed the diaper on the sleepy boy and prepared his blankets for the much-needed nap. Suddenly, just at the key moment of sleep, his eyes popped wide open, he rolled over off the bed, and ran into the next room. He did not take a nap under our watch that day. As days go, this one could have been better.

When we had first arrived in Hawaii, my daughter asked me, "What do you think about going to a luau on our final evening of the trip?"

"I have only been to one, many years ago, and don't have particularly fond memories of it," I responded.

But over the next several days, I noticed that she kept talking about luaus. Finally, on our last full day on the island, she told me, "Actually, I have already reserved a table for us, Dad; you will love it."

The time for the luau arrived. It was held at the Marriott Hotel, about a fifteen-minute drive from our condo. At least we all got to ride together in a van again. My son had done some research on the Marriott luau and was told that they close the food tables quickly. I noticed him eyeing the food tables frequently after we arrived. If you haven't been to a luau, it features a big dirt pit into which one or two whole dead pigs are placed and then covered with hot embers and cooked all day. Shortly after arriving at our table, Cole joined us with his white tee shirt and face covered with black soot. "My goodness, what happened to you?" my wife inquired.

"I found a big hole and crawled in with some pigs," he explained.

Suddenly, there was quite a commotion across the luau grounds. The food tables had opened and everyone, including us, began to rush to the table site. Apparently, the rumor was well-known. My son had loaded his plate with so much food that the piles were in danger of tipping over. "I don't want to miss out before they close the tables," he confided to me.

After dinner, a stage show took place with hula dancers, fire eaters, and other demonstrations of Hawaiian folklore. Although seated a fair distance away from the stage, I could see a commotion going on just below the stage itself. This area of lawn was roped off, but several little kids had apparently crawled under the ropes and turned it into a mosh pit scene with dancing, arm waving, and jumping around. Upon further squinting I saw that these kids were Caden, Emily, and Cole. It wasn't long before two things happened. Cole climbed onto the stage, and a security man showed up and cleared all the kids out.

The parking lot was dark, and we were tired. However, we had purchased a family photo from a professional photographer, and Caden was eager to see it right now. He climbed up on the side of the van with the door open and me in the driver's seat. I pulled out the photo to show him, but just then an incredible howl came out of his mouth. Cullen had accidently tripped the automatic door-closer button, closing the sliding van door on Caden's fingers. Again, I envisioned a long trip to an emergency room, and worse yet, the prospect of finishing our wonderful trip on a sad note. "Let's get some ice on the fingers," Cullen and Cynthia exclaimed.

We rushed back to the condo and iced the fingers. Miraculously, within about thirty minutes the fingers were fine, and Caden was watching TV.

In the morning we were all packed and said our goodbyes. I was singled out for special hugs. Our scorecard for the trip was: ten friends, zero serious injuries, and a happy Grumpa.

35 Morey Lane

Planning

In our family, a seventieth birthday is cause for celebration. Fortunately, as our family has two of the best event planners I have ever met, namely my wife and my daughter, we can do some pretty special things to honor a seventieth. My wife, Diane, celebrated her seventieth birthday last November, but it was unanimous that a family vacation should be planned for the following summer. In fact, that decision was actually made the summer before her seventieth birthday. As for location, the consensus was Nantucket. Diane and I visited Nantucket frequently when we lived in Boston years ago, and we have many great memories from the island. Our kids have also been there and love the wonderful New England summers.

By June, our planning team began a successful search for a rental in Nantucket. Plans were to make the trip a year from the upcoming August. The house selected was at 35 Morey Lane in the tiny town of Siasconset, generally known simply as 'Sconset. The good news finally arrived. The third week in August was available. Within a week of the news, everything was in place—deposit down°... airplane tickets purchased°... ready to go°... eleven months in advance.

Arrivals

Diane and I flew over to Nantucket from Boston, arriving about two in the afternoon. We were the first to arrive. Son James, his wife, Stacey and sons, Beau, three years old, and Cole, six years old, decided to take the ferry from Hyannis to the island. A text soon informed us that they were safely on their way and would arrive around five o'clock. Cynthia and her husband, Cullen, with their kids, Caden, seven years old, and Emily, six years old, were flying out to Boston from Seattle that day and were scheduled to fly over to Nantucket arriving around eight o'clock that evening. Diane said she would like to pick them up.

As Diane and I pulled up in front of the house, we were impressed by the size itself as well as by the big yard. The yard was immense, with grass-covered play areas on all sides of the house. The Jamaican housekeeping team was still on-site, finishing up the housecleaning from the last guests. The team leader was a cheerful young lady who seemed quite proud of 35 Morey Lane. She said they were almost ready for us and hoped we would enjoy the week there. The rest of the team looked less engaged and anxious to finish and go home for the weekend. Diane asked several mundane questions of one older lady with a scowl on her face. Only a grunt of, "I don't know," was forthcoming.

Soon they were done, and Diane and I inspected the premises. The house was everything we had hoped for, although a bit older than expected. We later learned that the house was close to one hundred years old. While some of the sliding doors seemed to have a tendency for sticking and occasionally coming off their tracks, this didn't seem to be a big problem. After a careful inspection, we couldn't find any real problems in this venerable and well-cared-for house. The day was hot and sticky, and we were pleased to find that the house had an efficient central air-conditioning unit. The compressor was located just outside one of the downstairs bedrooms.

Staking out turf was next, and Diane and I quickly claimed the master suite upstairs. James and Stacey, who by now had arrived with their kids, took some time to decide. Since Cynthia and family hadn't arrived, James and Stacey could have their choice of location. Finally, they decided on the two upstairs bedrooms. We could now look forward to a spaghetti dinner and the arrival of the rest of the family.

As night began to fall, we noted some distant lightning in the western sky. It was so far away that we could hear no thunder. We reminisced about summer storms, so frequent in the east during July and August. In some ways, we missed these storms, with warm rain that could soak you to the skin in about fifteen seconds. What we forgot about was the havoc these storms could play with transportation. Not long thereafter, the texts began. "Our flight is delayed due to weather," Cynthia announced.

It was now about eight o'clock and dark. The arrival time came and went. At eight thirty, Cynthia texted again, "We are looking bad for a flight, stay tuned."

We went ahead and ate our big spaghetti dinner with just the six of us. Finally, the expected message came from Cynthia. "Flight is cancelled, and we are searching for a hotel to bed down for the night. We are rebooked to arrive tomorrow at 10:00 a.m."

Sure enough, the next day dawned bright with all air travel on time. We met the rest of the clan with great cheer. Cynthia, Cullen, Caden, and Emily settled into the two remaining bedrooms, which were downstairs near the kitchen. I didn't mention the air-conditioner compressor, but after that night I noticed that the air-conditioner was not turned on during the rest of the visit.

The Supermarket

One of the obligatory jobs in a resort rental property is to stock up with food and drinks. Some knowledge of personal preferences is useful for the shopper but not critical. What is quite helpful is experience in dealing with the resort shopping procedure. The closest supermarket to our rental house was about twenty minutes by car, called Stop & Shop. "I'll come along and help with the shopping," I volunteered to Diane, happy to help and hoping to make sure I got my favorite items in the cart.

As we entered the packed parking lot, I had a sense of déjà vu. Cars were darting here and there, spaces were hard to find, and harried shoppers were pushing huge shopping carts around the lot at breakneck speed. "Wow, let's be careful in here," I exclaimed.

"Just stick with me; I know how to handle this," Diane replied.

As we entered the Stop & Shop, it was clear that this was the big time. Four different styles of shopping carts were available. The regular metal grid cart was front and center, but in addition Stop & Shop offered a plastic, contoured cart, which I had never seen before. Also, a kids' theme cart was available, with animal-shaped seats and bright colors. Most disturbing to me, however, was the wide-bodied model. This was a takeoff on the regular metal-grid cart but made to hold almost twice the grocery capacity. I envisioned aisle blockades forming when more than one of these carts showed up at the same time.

As soon as we entered the shopping area, it was clear that there were rookies and veterans. It was easy to spot rookie vacation shoppers. In most cases they were men pushing carts for their wives, and these men looked as though they had not been frequent shoppers in any supermarket. Uniformly, they appeared tense, with faces drawn tight. Their cart management was tentative, often courteous to other shoppers, giving way to challenges for the same space. Many of the rookies seemed to take a shelter-in-place approach. This technique involved finding a cart-size nook behind a large stack of food cases. Importantly, this nook needed to be out of the main flow of traffic. The rookie would nestle his cart into the nook and ask if his wife could carry items over to the cart. This plan worked for only so long however, and it needed to be abandoned when the wife moved on to distant aisles.

Then there were the veteran shoppers. These people moved fast, seemed to know exactly where things were located, were aggressive to the point of being rude, and never gave way to an oncoming shopping cart. In observing the veterans, I estimated that they could get their shopping done in about 50 percent less time than the rookies. The veterans did share one quality with the rookies. All shoppers had the same "let's get this over with and get back to vacation" look on their faces.

I had noticed that as we entered the store, a disproportionate number of expensive specialty items were on display. Fancy baked goods, such as layered chocolate cakes and beautifully frosted cookies, were especially tempting. Diane put several items into the cart, saying, "These are resort prices." As we moved deeper into the store, she perked up. "Look, here are the normal-priced breads and cookies," she said.

I then saw her remove the expensive baked goods from the cart and place them randomly on shelves nearby. "What are you doing? Aren't you supposed to take those things back to their spot in the front of the store?" I asked.

"It is too hard to fight my way back there, and besides, I am annoyed by the way they put these overpriced items just inside the front door," she replied.

The rest of the shopping seemed to settle into fairly routine choices. We were careful to load up on whole-wheat bread rather than white bread. Our families told us on several occasions that they avoided white bread because it was made from refined flour and was boring. In fact, they said they wouldn't give their children white bread at all. I love white bread and successfully lobbied Diane to put one loaf in the cart just for me. Diane, it turns out, doesn't seem to care about this issue and will eat anything. Finally, we were finished with the shopping phase of the project.

The grand finale of resort supermarket shopping is the checkout line. Here, overloaded shopping carts come together like Sherman tanks, often with items dropping off onto the floor. The rookies hate this part and uniformly sport expressions of both fear and surprise on their faces. "I wonder how long this will take?" I mumbled to Diane.

"Don't worry about it," she said confidently. "Just stick close to me with that cart."

I was amazed by her maneuvering as she picked out the best line and finessed her way toward the front. Still, with time on my hands as we inched forward, I began a new game called "Guess how much the total tab will be for that cart of groceries." After missing guesses on several carts, always by low-balling, I caught on. These were all going to be big tabs, often well exceeding $250. Our tab was $278.

The Dead Owls

Walking is a big pastime in Nantucket. Thirty-five Morey Lane was located within an easy ten-minute walk of the cute village of 'Sconset. A weatherworn, wooden village market, a sandwich shop, and a small liquor store clustered around the village center. Bicycle and car traffic was directed around a rotary marker enhanced with a center flagpole sporting the American Flag. Along the oceanfront road to the village, you pass a resort/restaurant called Summer House. The main building housed a hotel and formal restaurant, while the ocean side of the road offered an informal beach-style restaurant called Summer House Bistro. You could reach the Bistro by descending a long stairway to a patio with a pool, bar, patio furniture, and tables. It looked inviting, and it wasn't long before the common wisdom among the family was that it would be great to have dinner in this informal and fun-looking place. "I'll drop by and make a reservation next time I walk by," I promised.

The next day, I walked by the Summer House Bistro at around two in the afternoon and descended the stairway. A pretty young woman with dark hair greeted me with a big smile. "Can I help you, sir?" she chirped.

I detected an Eastern European accent. This was no surprise, as Nantucket is a popular destination for Romanian and Bulgarian students to work during summer vacations. "Yes, I would like to make a reservation for tomorrow night around six p.m. for ten people. We have four children and six adults." I explained.

"That's great! What is your name? she replied.

"My name is Jim," I answered.

"Jim what?" she said.

Trying to keep things on the island-informal side, I just said, "Jim P."

"Okay, thanks," she replied.

I looked down at the reservation book as she carefully wrote, "Jim Pee."

As our family of ten gathered around the dinner table the next evening, a commotion flared. The kids were shoving one another with elbows, pushing one another out of seats, and generally being rude to one another. The issue it seemed was that every kid wanted to sit by Beau. I sat at the far end of the table, well away from three-year-old Beau, who tends to spill water and jump up and down. I worried that we might just be too noisy and disruptive for this relaxed patio restaurant. "Don't worry. I have kids of my own. I get it," said the waitress who had just arrived.

This was somewhat reassuring, but it was still early. I remembered past dinners that seemed calm at first only to be disrupted suddenly by a glass mustard jar smashing to the floor. "Could we get some drinks?" I implored.

"No problem, we will get drinks out here as soon as possible, and get a food order in for the kids," she said with an understanding manner.

Maybe this would work out after all.

Not so fast. It wasn't more than five minutes before the kids were up and out of their seats. "We have decided to do some exploring," Caden announced. He had been appointed spokesperson for the kids.

Drinks were thankfully just arriving, and Stacey grabbed her drink, which was in a plastic cup, and said, "I will trail them."

After some time passed, I began to relax. The Mai Tai was helping. The kids were still gone. Life was good.

Suddenly, I felt a violent tugging on my shirt sleeve. I looked over and didn't see anyone. Then I looked down and saw an unexpected sight. There was Beau with a flushed face and eyes rounder and bigger than I have ever seen on a three-year-old boy. "Grandpa, Grandpa, come see the dead owls," he stammered with excitement.

"What! Do you even know what an owl looks like?" I asked, hoping this was all a dream.

No more discussion was allowed; it was get up and go see dead owls. I noticed that Stacey was with the newly returned kids and was shaking her head in agreement. It looked like I must go. I did take along my Mai Tai in the plastic cup. I rightly assumed that I would need this drink.

We walked in single file from the patio, through tall grass, on a path to the beach. Beau was in the lead, followed by the other kids. Stacey was the only other adult who wanted to go out and see the dead owls. I brought up the rear of the line. After a short walk along the beach, we came upon the dead owls. Beau and the other kids began dancing round them in a circle, much like an Indian war dance.

Indeed, there were two dead birds, feathers and all. One bird looked recently deceased, as it had a full body and lots of feathers. The other bird looked long gone. Other than some scraggly feathers and a beak, there wasn't much left. I had no way to tell what kind of birds they were and was suspect of the owl identification. How many owls were there hanging around the beach in Nantucket? "How do you know these are owls?" I inquired to anyone who could answer.

"Oh, they're owls alright," Stacey quickly replied.

The evidence leading to the identification as owls was never disclosed. But I knew then and there that these were indeed dead owls.

After returning to the dinner table, I could see that I had missed some excitement. My son, James, was looking gloomy and showed me what had happened. Squarely in the middle of his most expensive shirt for the trip sat a large wet red spot. "What happened?" I inquired in my most sympathetic voice.

"Well, I needed to ask the manager a question and finally found her." he explained. "As I approached her, I noticed that she was eating something. As I got closer, I saw that it was a raw tomato. Suddenly, as we were chatting, a large fountain of tomato juice squirted out of the tomato, just as she was taking a bite."

Driving in Nantucket Town

Located at the other end of Nantucket Island, about twenty miles from our village of 'Sconset, is the town of Nantucket. Nantucket Town is a relic of the nineteenth century, when the whaling industry was thriving in New England. Read *Moby Dick* for more details about whaling. Very little architectural change has taken place in Nantucket Town, and the streets remain narrow, winding, and paved in stones. Needless to say, driving a modern car around the town is challenging, and parking is almost nonexistent.

The kids had decided to give Diane and me a date night. We accepted and made reservations for a nice restaurant in Nantucket Town. Since Diane is our best driver, she took the wheel for the trip. As we approached the center of town, it was apparent that things were as crowded, tight, and difficult as ever. "I remember a good parking lot right in the center of town," she told me.

"Great, go for it," I responded hopefully.

We soon reached the lot, which was located just across the street from the wharfs and ferry docks. It was full, but Diane has innate parking karma, so we circled around the street and back into the lot for another try. After no joy, we again approached the lot exit, but this time the already tight street was further narrowed by a large parked bus. "Careful," I cautioned.

Just as we made the tight turn onto the street, a metal-on-cement scraping sound emitted from the right front of the car. I looked out from the passenger seat to see several tourists shaking their heads collectively and pointing at us. "Uh-oh," said Diane. "What happened?"

"Let's find a different place to park," I suggested. "Then we can assess the damage."

After parking in a faraway neighborhood spot, I got out and looked. Sure enough, the right front fender just in front of the right tire was bent outward, away from the body. It wasn't really too much of a bend, probably about an inch or less from the normal body surface. But it was easy to see, and despite some energetic pushing, I could not get the fender to bend back and stay in place. "Well, I guess this is on us," I said sadly. "This car is rented under James's name, so we need to make sure he isn't stuck with the damages when he turns it in," I added.

Diane had already figured this out and was planning how we could go about tending to this. During our dinner, which was going to cost a lot more than we had figured, we decided we would take the car to a body shop first thing in the morning. We would not tell James until we had things worked out.

The next morning, we were up bright and early, and I was on the phone to the Nantucket Auto Body shop. "Bring it over, and we will look it over," said the woman on the phone. "And don't forget the registration."

The Nantucket Auto Body shop was a different world from the rest of the island. Instead of the perfectly turned-out preppy tourists and smiling clerks in their print summer dresses and sandals, we were in a world of tattooed men, dirty tee shirts, and greasy hands. I went into the office and Diane waited in the car. The man in line in front of me asked the desk clerk, "Can I get my oil changed today?"

"No," she said.

"Well, how about tomorrow?" he asked.

"Nope, this is our busy season, and you need an appointment," she explained blandly.

"Okay, how about an appointment sometime this week?" he implored.

"Nothing available," she said without any sign of empathy.

He left, and I was next. For some reason, the woman was more helpful for me. Facing a thousand-dollar body repair job probably didn't hurt.

"I'll copy this registration and then send the boss out to look it over," she promised.

As I waited by the car, I saw the boss lumbering across the parking area. He was of medium height, considerably overweight, had tattoos on both arms, and wore a blue tee shirt smeared with grease and oil. "Okay, what happened?" he asked us.

I showed him the bent fender. He continued the inspection and asked, "What about this?"

To my horror, he had looked below the bumper on the right and found an even bigger dent. "Oh boy, I didn't notice that," I exclaimed.

As dollar signs began to mount up in my mind, the boss asked, "Is this a rental car?"

"Yes," I said meekly, wondering if that made a difference.

"What company?" he asked.

"Windmill," I responded.

"Oh, forget it then. They take their cars somewhere else. I can't touch this."

We were really down. As we drove back to 35 Morey, we decided that we should just tell James what happened and to let us know what we owe him. Upon arrival at the house, we saw James in the yard. "Hey, where have you guys been?" he said cheerfully.

"James, we have bad news," I said. "We damaged your rental car when we were in Nantucket Town last night. But don't worry; we will reimburse you for whatever the rental company charges."

"Show me what happened," James said.

Upon inspecting the bent fender and body dent under the bumper, he said, "Don't worry about that stuff. That was there when I picked up the car, and I pointed it out on the rental contract."

The Russian Goodbye

When Diane and I attend a large cocktail party, I am usually the first to express the desire to leave. Diane generally agrees in principle, but while I gather my coat, thank the hosts, and stand by the door, I typically see Diane making little if any true attempt to leave. Instead, she circles the room saying goodbye to almost everyone, telling them she is leaving now. It can mount up to fifteen to twenty minutes before she finally joins me at the door and I pull her outside. This promise to leave without really leaving is fondly known as the Russian goodbye. Toward the end of our wonderful week in Nantucket, I unexpectedly experienced a situation that reminded me of a Russian goodbye.

A family trip is generally a total family trip, meaning activities are planned for, agreed on, and participated in by everyone. Exceptions can occur when a smaller group with a common interest undertakes a separate activity, with, of course, the agreement of all concerned. A men's-only activity was planned for Thursday morning. For months, son James had been looking forward to one round of golf with me. He had researched courses, proposed them to me, and we finally agreed that a local nine-hole course called Old Nantucket Golf Course would be perfect. This course was opened in 1899, and not a lot of change has taken place there since. Greens fees and club rentals were dirt cheap, and the course was only a ten-minute drive from Morey Lane. Diane suggested that we invite Cullen to join the father-son pair and make it a threesome. Best of all, the women had unanimously agreed to let us men off-site alone for a nine-hole round.

James was to be the leader for the group, selecting departure time and which car to take. We all agreed the night before that getting an early start would be a good idea. The girls listened carefully to our planning. Their morning needed to match up with our plans. "Let's see if we can get going by eight in the morning," James suggested.

Thursday dawned with filtered sun. Mist hung over the ground as I arose, ready for an early departure. As I descended the stairs around seven thirty, I noticed that Diane was not around. James was already up, so I asked him where she was. "Oh, she just left for the Stop & Shop; she said everyone was asking for white bread and we had run out," he explained.

"But we can't leave until she returns," I noted. "That wouldn't be fair to the others."

Diane had told me the night before that the women had agreed that they should all be home together while we were gone so that no one got stuck with all the kids.

"Don't worry, she said she won't be long," James explained. "We can still plan for an early departure."

I was skeptical, but I began making myself some toast and a bowl of Cheerios. I noted the absence of white bread, further darkening my mood.

By now it was 7:50 a.m. and no Diane. Out of the corner of my eye I saw Cynthia pulling out of the driveway on a bicycle. "Wait!" I called out as she departed.

I guess she didn't hear me, and we were now down two of the three women. "James, this isn't looking good for an eight a.m. departure," I complained.

Cullen had joined us in the kitchen, and he agreed that things were slipping. James revised his departure estimate to 8:30 a.m. sharp. I was all dressed, standing by the door, with no movement by others.

At about eight fifteen, Stacey appeared in the kitchen wearing her jogging outfit. "I won't be too long, boys," she promised as she sprinted out the back door.

I turned to our leader, "Okay, when are we really leaving?"

I was now measuring the departure time in hours not minutes. We were now down three of the three women, and I didn't see this situation coming.

You Can Teach an Old Dog New Tricks

One of the true treats of any New England vacation is to have a lobster feed. The local New England lobsters are plentiful, cheap, and fresh as can be. Along with drawn butter and lemon to dip the lobster meat; crisp, warm French bread; and perhaps some fresh summer ears of corn, it can't be beat. Our family vacation would conclude with a lobster feed at 35 Morey on Friday night. Diane ordered the lobsters ahead of time at Stop & Shop to be sure we had no last-minute disappointments.

In fact, as Friday was our last day, we packed our schedule with fun things. We stopped at a place called Cisco Brewery for lunch. This place was only ten minutes from Cisco Beach, our favorite beach among several we had visited during the week. The so-called Brewery was much more than a brewery, as it included live music, several food trucks selling all kinds of fast food, and a stand with two burly tattooed guys shucking fresh oysters for sale. "Get a big order; I really love oysters," said Cullen as I headed over to get in line.

After lunch, we spent three hours at Cisco Beach, surfing and sunning. We were tan, sandy, and tired at the end of the day. On the way back, Diane and I stopped at the Stop & Shop to pick up our lobsters.

Back at Morey, we all showered and made preparations for a big dinner. The kids were fascinated by the living and lively lobsters. They didn't ask many questions, however. I am an expert at boiling live lobsters, having been responsible for that job at a restaurant during my high school days. I filled two large pots with water and added a lot of salt and vinegar. It was still several hours before dinnertime, but it does take considerable time to get these giant pots up to a boil. We opened chilled white wine and laid out crackers and cheese.

I can honestly say that over my many years as a physician, I have encountered and treated most common medical disorders. Sore throats, coughs, belly aches, headaches—I knew them all and how to deal with them. I would be surprised to come across a common ailment about which I could still learn something new. But I was about to be surprised.

"Where is Cullen?" I asked Cynthia as I saw her scurry across the kitchen with a worried look on her face.

She didn't answer and disappeared into their bedroom near the kitchen. Come to think of it, I hadn't seen Cullen since I finished my shower an hour ago. That, plus the look on Cynthia's face suggested that something was wrong. Cullen is always a good party guy and should have been standing in the kitchen with a glass of wine or a beer in his hand.

"Dad, could you come in here and look at Cullen?" Cynthia asked, sticking her head out of their bedroom doorway.

As I entered the bedroom, I was taken aback. Cullen's shirt was off, and his body was doubled up into the fetal position as he lay writhing in agony on the bed. His face was red. He was down for the count. "What is wrong?" I said in my most doctor-like voice.

"Terrible stomach pains," he grunted.

I told him to roll over onto his back as best he could. I felt his abdomen and found nothing remarkable. He was cool, not febrile. My immediate concern about appendicitis was alleviated.

"I think I got a bad oyster," he groaned.

Certainly, the timing and the symptoms were consistent with a case of food poisoning. I recalled Cullen enjoying a fair share of oysters at lunch. Getting a bad oyster is kind of like Russian roulette. Only one oyster among twenty may be bad. It is the unlucky person who gets the bad one.

"Alright, just rest if you can. This usually takes several hours to get better," I tried to reassure.

I knew that food poisoning often lasts much longer than a few hours, but I wanted to be as encouraging as possible.

I left Cynthia in the room with Cullen and went back to the kitchen to join the party. A few minutes later, I noticed Cynthia at the far side of the kitchen looking through the liquor cabinet. She grabbed a bottle of vodka and headed back to the bedroom. "What's going on?" I asked.

"Oh, Cullen said he thinks vodka will help him," she explained.

My expert medical knowledge knew this to be ridiculous, but since it shouldn't hurt him, why interfere?

It was now thirty minutes to countdown for the lobster boil. Pots were reaching a boil and bread was in the oven. We all felt bad that Cullen would miss the climactic event of our week, but he could be with us in spirit. Suddenly the door to his bedroom sprang open, Cullen jumped out fully dressed, and with a smile on his face said, "Okay, guys, let's party!"

The vodka had knocked out the food poisoning in less than an hour.

Part 1

Babysitting in Seattle

I had plenty of advance notice—several months, in fact. My wife and I were going to do our daughter, Cynthia, and son-in-law the favor of babysitting their two kids for a weekend at their home in Seattle. Meanwhile, Cynthia and Cullen would fly down to San Francisco, rent a car, and tour Napa Valley. This was to celebrate Cynthia's fortieth birthday. We had survived a similar babysitting weekend at our own home with Caden and Emily about two years ago. The fact that the kids were now two years older, namely five and six, eased any anxiety I might have had.

We arrived at their home on Mercer Island, a suburb of Seattle, late on a sunny Thursday afternoon. Both kids were just coming home from school, and upon seeing Grandma and Grandpa they raced up to us and gave us big hugs. It seemed that Emily had something she wanted to share. She began waving her hands and jumping around. So I paid attention to her. She then informed me that "I can make milk come out of my nose."

I acknowledged that this was hard to do and hoped to see her perform this trick during my visit. I even went so far as to tell her that I could make a blueberry come out of my nose. At that, my wife began frowning and moving in my direction.

The next morning, Cynthia and Cullen were off to the airport at the crack of dawn, and my wife, Diane, and I were officially on duty. A fairly major squabble occurred when it was time to go to school. Since the school is only one mile away, the option of walking is always open. Walking would be under the watchful eye of an adult. Caden elected the walking option, but Emily wanted to ride. Compromise was not in the cards. The incredible outcome was that Diane loaded Emily into the car and followed Caden by car as he ran/walked to school. The rest of Friday was uneventful.

Saturday is a big day for five- and six-year-old kids in suburbia. Emily had a ballet practice at 10:00 a.m. followed by a T-ball practice at noon. Caden had an important baseball game at 9:30 a.m. We had been briefed carefully on how to locate these events before Cynthia left for California. My assignment was to transport Caden to and from his baseball game. I looked over the driving instructions and frankly was worried. They reminded me of a maze, and I'm known for getting lost in mazes. I then searched Google Maps and was still not sure how to find this place. To make matters worse, Cynthia had told me that not only was Caden not to be late, but that his coach demanded that all the kids arrive at least fifteen minutes before the game.

I studied the instructions again: follow Isle Crest for four miles, then turn left on SE Twenty-Seventh Street, turn right on Seventy-Sixth Avenue SE, followed by left on SE Twenty-Fourth Street, then a right on Seventy-Second Avenue SE. When I pulled out of the driveway at 8:45 a.m., I was sure I had built in some get lost time. Hoping for a little assistance, as we started out, I asked Caden if the games were held at the same place each week. Caden seemed to be unfamiliar with where we were headed. He finally confessed that though his games were always at this same field, he didn't know exactly where it was located. Happily, I found the general area, and we pulled into a four-block-long parking lot. "We need to find the trail," Caden informed me.

"Do you know where it is?" I asked.

"Sure, just follow me," he replied.

At last I could relax. We were now at 9:20 a.m., and the game began at 9:30 a.m. Things were admittedly beginning to slip a bit, but at least I would deliver Caden to the field ahead of game time.

Not so fast. Caden made several wrong turns and began to squint. I have never seen him squint before. To make matters worse, I noticed that his mouth was drawn tight. And he was beginning to shake ever so gently. Now he began an exercise of trial and error. He would start down one trail only to return and head down another. Finally, after wandering about a quarter of a mile from where we parked, he started jumping up and down and waving his arms. "Let's go, let's go," he yelled as he ran off.

This was the one, and he topped it off by saying he was going to take a shortcut. Suddenly he was gone. I held my breath. He suddenly appeared about fifty feet down the trail, and I ran to catch up with him. "Are you sure this is the right trail?" I asked as he scampered off again.

"Yes," he shouted.

We reached the end of the trail and lo and behold, there was the baseball diamond. It was now 9:28 a.m. I told him to run over to his team, which was already in a pregame huddle. So Caden did make it by game time, although I hadn't really fulfilled my assignment. Then again, things could have been worse. I stayed clear of the coach as he assigned starting positions and sent Caden to right field. In my day, playing right field was like being in Siberia, but Caden ran out without a fuss.

As I neared the baseball field, I noticed something foreign to my expectations. Standing on the pitcher's mound was a father and next to him a peculiar-looking contraption. It turned out that this was something called a mechanical pitcher. The apparatus stands about four feet tall and has a lever-like arm with a basket on the tip. The father loads the ball into the basket and then triggers the device. The lever arm springs forward, catapulting the ball in the direction of home plate, where the batter waits. If the pitch looks good, the batter tries to hit the ball.

I surmised that the theory of using this device is to deliver a consistent pitch and allow the young batters to expect a hittable ball. In practice, the device needed constant adjusting by the father to try and deliver hittable balls. Every once in a while, the father would just start pitching himself.

I haven't attended a Little League baseball game in many years. I had forgotten how many interesting things one can casually observe. Next time you attend this type of game, watch the goings-on in the dugout area. This is where the team members are supposed to stay when their team is batting and their own turn hasn't arrived yet. I took a hard look at Caden and noticed that he was standing quietly by a teammate named Grogen. I knew his friend's name because *Grogen* was emblazoned on the back of his jersey. The boys appeared engrossed in the game and were not conversing. I just happened to look down and noticed that Caden was standing squarely on top of Grogen's right foot.

It was hard not to notice the woman who was busily doing things in the dugout. She was of medium height and had brown hair and just enough body fat to emphasize the curves. She looked to be about thirty or so. She seemed to be making every effort to assist the players. For example, she struggled to help the catcher put on his special protective gear. When this was not successful, a fourteen-year-old boy with a knit ski cap came by and lent a hand. "I've never done this before," she explained.

I finally asked one of the spectators who that woman was. "Oh, that is Huggie's mom, and she is the dugout mom for the week," was the response. "That is a tough job for the moms," the spectator added.

I was later informed that Huggie's mom used to be an actress in Hollywood.

Given the informal and close confines of a Little League ball field, you can get quite close to the action. For a while, I stood within five feet of home plate to watch the batter's form. One player by the name of Bazie was known to be the best batter on the team. Unfortunately, while I watched, he struck out. As he shuffled away from the plate back to the dugout, I heard him mutter under his breath, "That hasn't happened for a while."

Just then I felt a tug on my shirt, looked down, and there was Caden. "Can you buy a cookie for me?" he said.

"Where would I find a cookie?" I asked.

"Right there," he explained.

I followed his directions and sure enough, I discovered a card table set up in the shade under a tree upon which an array of snacks and drinks offered themselves to the players and spectators. Cookies were in prominent display. Tacked to the front of the table was a homemade sign reading Bake for the Cure. There was no explanation of what was hopefully going to be cured. I found a dollar and contributed to the cause.

As I waited for Caden to select his cookie, I noticed something out of the corner of my eye. It was white and was moving across the pavement. I looked down to find a small baby crawling around. Based upon the pink hat, I presumed this to be a little girl. The crawler was picking up scraps of food as she crawled and putting them into her mouth. I remember in medical school being taught that raw exposure to the environment would toughen up your immune system for later life. I was now witnessing this in real time.

Finally, the game ended. It appeared that the end of a game in this league is determined by time, not innings. "Who won the game?" I asked Caden.

"We don't keep score," he replied.

This did and didn't make sense to me. On the one hand, I understood the attempt to keep things low-key at this young age. On the other hand, where is the learning about competition and the importance of winning? What is the motivation to work hard and get better? I wondered if this was just me, or were these kids really missing a life lesson. Quickly I realized that I wasn't going to solve this issue and moved on in my head.

As we walked back to the car, we stopped to watch a game being played by much older boys. They were really good. I knew they all wanted to win and that they were keeping score. I pointed this out to Caden, and he nodded his head.

After reaching the car, I thought about reviewing the driving instructions in reverse order but decided that this wouldn't be necessary. Once I began the drive home, my confidence was quickly shaken when I began passing unfamiliar landmarks. I stopped and took out my instructions. "Are we lost?" Caden asked.

Before offering a casual response, such as maybe, or yes, I remembered that a little kid is often unsure of where he is once he gets a long way from home. If the adult is also lost, then serious anxiety can set in. I also thought about some fairy tales, such as *Hansel and Gretel*, which emphasize the dreadful consequences when little children become lost. "I missed my turn, but I see exactly how to go back and find the right street," I explained, proud of this perfect combination of honesty and reassurance.

With all the scheduled Saturday events completed, it was free time for the rest of the day. Caden quickly picked up his iPad and began watching a movie. After an hour, I asked him if he wanted to go for a walk or bike ride. "No, I'm okay," he said.

After another hour, I inquired about how much time his parents allow for sitting around and watching movies. "They let me watch as long as I want," he mumbled without looking at me.

This sounded fishy, so I said that I would like for him to turn off the iPad and join me for some basketball in the driveway. "It is a nice afternoon, and we both need some fresh air," I explained.

Emily heard what we were up to and asked if she could join. My wife also came outside as an observer.

We started with a simple and quiet game called H-O-R-S-E. This game requires that you make the same shot that your predecessor makes. If you miss, you acquire a letter, starting with H. The first person to have all five letters is the loser°… the HORSE.

Finally, I asked if they wanted to take me on in a real basketball game with two kids versus Grandpa. This sounded like more action, and we quickly made up our rules. Once one team makes a basket, the other team automatically gets the ball.

It soon became evident that the two-kid team was well-organized. Emily played defense exclusively, while Caden would take the shots. This made sense since Emily was not able to throw the ball as high as the basket. And she played an extremely aggressive brand of defense. This consisted of staying right in front of me at all times with both arms outstretched, continuously pushing into my stomach. Meanwhile Caden was free to run at will and shoot baskets.

It was clear that if I had any chance at all, I would need to shove Emily aside. This might be a risky move, but my competitive juices were flowing, even against a five-year-old.

I made the mistake of trying a shove Emily, and then it happened. Our witness was my wife, who said that she saw it all.

Suddenly I felt my rubber sandal catch on something on the paved driveway. I was quickly off my feet, hurtling through the air. Since Emily had been directly in front of me, I was about to land right on top of her. She would be the filling in a human-concrete sandwich. Just in the nick of time, my left hand hit the driveway, and I was able to push myself off to the side, avoiding a really serious incident. Emily was barely touched. I had deep cuts in my elbow and finger and a massive bruise on my knee. Emily started a *pro forma* cry, although she wasn't hurt. When she saw real blood on me, however, she stopped.

A lesson was learned, which was to never play driveway basketball wearing flimsy rubber sandals. But other lessons were also clear. I need to be careful about competitive juices and the desire to win. These are little kids. Put it in perspective.

Sunday arrived, and the excitement of Emily's annual ballet recital filled the air. This recital serves as the culmination of many months of ballet lessons and practice in the community recreation center. Dozens of little girls wake up this day and know that all that hard work is about to pay off. Parents, siblings, grandparents, and friends of all ages are expected to show up at the local high school auditorium and support the dancers. My daughter and son-in-law had timed their return from California to allow them to attend the 2:00 p.m. event. My wife and I were to depart that afternoon from Seattle airport at 5:00 p.m., which would allow for us to attend the first part of the show. The stars were aligned for a big day.

The girls were to be at the high school at noon, two hours ahead of curtain time. There, makeup would be applied in layers and hair carefully put into a tight tieback with a bun on top. This was apparently an eagerly awaited part of the proceedings. Shortly before two o'clock, Diane, Caden, and I arrived at the high school auditorium. As planned, Cynthia and Cullen had arrived back from their trip and were there to meet us.

Nestling into my seat, I looked over what appeared to be a pretty long program. I counted fifteen separate dance numbers with an intermission planned midway through the program. Emily's piece was the last before the intermission and was labeled preschool dancers group. Of note, the dance pieces on the program were not arranged by youngest to oldest groups. This random ordering made it a bit of luck that we could see Emily dance before we needed to make our early departure for the airport.

The dancing was not bad. Some rather husky sixth-grade girls danced energetically. They did not meet the stereotype of a ballerina; they had trouble getting up on their toes, but they were clearly proud of their performance. I couldn't help but think that this was probably close to the last time they would be on a stage in a ballerina role. But that may be okay, I mused, as they could carry away confidence that might stand them in good stead later on.

Emily's group was really cute and did well. At first, from where I was seated, these little ones all looked alike. They formed an almost perfect circle, joined hands, and began circling counterclockwise. Suddenly I spotted Emily. She was doing a particularly good job circling. I was proud to be a grandpa. "Way to go, Emily," I whispered under my breath.

After about an hour and fifteen minutes, we reached intermission. The program was just barely half over.

As Diane and I sat in the taxi on the way to the airport, we reflected on the weekend. Despite not being on time for some scheduled events, and despite my accident on the driveway, we agreed that we were getting pretty good at babysitting. We might do it again someday.

Part 2

I'm in Trouble

"Dad, I'm really upset with you!" my daughter exclaimed into my phone.

It was exactly two weeks after my wife and I had spent the weekend in Seattle babysitting our six- and seven-year-old grandchildren. I hoped this wasn't something left over from our weekend. But of course it was.

"Did you tell Emily about two little girls covered with blood and running around saying 'REDRUM?'" she asked.

"Uh, maybe," I stammered. "Why?"

"When I tried to put Emily to bed tonight, she told me she couldn't sleep because Grandpa had told her such scary things. She specifically told me about the blood-covered little girls," my daughter said in a voice at least one octave above normal. "Emily must have had this bottled up inside for two weeks and let it out tonight."

I then remembered that in the context of discussing scary movies, a subject that I brought up, I said that *The Shining* was probably the scariest movie that I've seen. I related the scene where the ghosts of the Grady twins, two young girls previously killed by their father, appear covered with blood as they proceed down the hall of the Overlook Hotel. I then changed my voice and imitated the soundtrack repeating the word "REDRUM, REDRUM" (MURDER spelled backward).

"My God, why in the world would you tell a six-year-old girl that stuff?" my daughter reprimanded. "Don't you know that their little minds are like sponges? They absorb this stuff, and it keeps coming back. Frankly, I don't know if I can trust you around the kids."

So, according to my daughter, I had screwed the babysitting weekend up, and now I was clearly on probation. I had a sinking feeling. The sense of accomplishment shared with my wife two weeks ago in the taxi was flying away. Would I even be allowed around the kids again without direct supervision?

My daughter also called my wife. Later, when I timidly asked my wife whether Cynthia had mentioned that she and I had spoken—hoping that perhaps Cynthia would keep this between just the two of us—my wife replied, "Yes, I spoke to her." Then she added, "I just have to ask you, 'Are you crazy?'"

How and why did I get into this mess? What possessed me to purposely tell Emily such scary things?

I have spent a good deal of time thinking about this. I do not underestimate the seriousness of family impact here. And above all, I will not attempt to offer excuses for my action, just apologies.

However, after considerable thought, I do have a plausible explanation for why I felt that telling a little kid something scary might be acceptable. Having been subjected to many examples of this, including horror movies, frightening clowns, and gruesome fairy tales during my childhood, discussing scary things with Emily didn't seem too unusual. I have always been aware of and fascinated by the world of mystery, darkness, danger, and evil. I confronted many scary movies and stories in my childhood, and I believe I became a stronger and better person for learning how to deal with such things. In fact, I think I enjoyed being scared at times. Perhaps I wanted my grandchildren to be introduced to this other world and learn how to process and deal with being scared.

In fact, it turns out that for centuries it has been common in Western civilization to purposely scare the bejesus out of little kids. I realize that West Coast, USA, in 2015 is not the land of European ogres, trolls, dwarfs, witches, evil stepmothers, or talking animals. However, raised in the 1940s, I encountered a daily diet of colorfully illustrated fairy-tale books. These children's books were filled with grotesque pictures of unspeakable creatures. Talking anthropomorphic animals, such as mice, horses, pigs, and especially wolves, were commonplace. Torture, abuse, false imprisonment, unexplained deaths, and cannibalism were the norm.

To exam the tradition of scaring kids, let's look at two phenomena: clowns and fairy tales.

Clowns are an ironic example. First created by circuses in the eighteenth century, clowns were purported to be funny and of special delight for little children. But in reality, clowns are just the opposite. One of the scariest encounters I had as a youngster was when my parents took me to meet Bozo the Clown. Bozo the Clown was created in the early 1940s, and by the late 1940s had become the mascot of Capital Records. As a promotion, a local record store featured a chance to meet Bozo in person and maybe even let him touch you. Imagine my horror in seeing a man-size person, but with a white face and huge red mouth. I joined in with the other kids at the record store by howling and begging to get out.

At least I could get out. My poor son, during his early years, was forced to live with a large, hard-to-see clown that inhabited the corner of his bedroom at night. Only my son could see this clown, who was said to have a particularly large number of buttons on his clothes. He didn't come every night, but he came often enough that we visited a child psychiatrist in an attempt to expunge the clown. That didn't work, but after my son reached about six years old, the clown stopped visiting.

Fear of clowns is well-known. There is actually a term for fear of clowns, *coulrophobia.* Yet clowns persist to this day and are still supposed to delight children. A fair amount of research has been done to document and quantify this fear. For example, a professor at Cal State Hayward found that "Young children are very reactive to a familiar body type with an unfamiliar face." In evaluating what would be cheerful wall decorations and images in a new pediatric ward, Dr. Penny Curtis at University of Sheffield in England discovered "that clowns are universally disliked by children. Some found the clown images frightening."

Perhaps the greatest source of scary and outrageous tales for little children comes from the centuries-old tradition of European fairy tales. These stories, some of which would not be allowed to reach publication today, have been unapologetically related to children of all ages—and in some cases celebrated with nationalistic pride. The justification for the tales is generally that they teach important lessons. And who can deny that following instructions from parents, being honest, being careful with strangers, and being industrious rather than lazy are worthy life teachings? The method of making the lessons sink in, however, in many cases is to tie the lesson to horrific situations. Being eaten by a talking wolf, or cremating an old woman in an iron oven while listening to her screams until she dies, is hardly the way I would chose to get lessons across. That notwithstanding, these fairy tales remain for some an import medium for doing so.

If I think about a few of the tales told to me as a child, I can reexperience, perhaps, the impact the stories made on a six-year-old boy in 1949.

The Pied Piper of Hamelin

This is a short and simple tale that dates back to the thirteenth century. The small town of Hamelin was infested by rats. One day, a gaily dressed (pied) stranger came to town carrying a musical instrument called a pipe. He told the mayor that for a fee, he would play his magical pipe and lead the rats out of town to their deaths. A deal was made, and the piper indeed led the rats out of town to a nearby river to see them all drowned. Later, the mayor reneged on his promise and would not pay the piper. Subsequently, on a religious holiday, as all adults were in church, the piper reappeared, and upon playing his pipe, led all 130 of the town's children out of town into a cave. The children were never seen again. Actually, one crippled child who was left behind was able to explain to the puzzled and frightened adults what had happened.

Clear message: lie and cheat and bad things happen. Even worse, in this case it happens to the children instead of the adults, who caused the mess.

The Three Little Pigs

This is an old English tale first published in the 1840s. The pigs are anthropomorphic and speak. The mother pig sent her three little boy pigs out into the world to seek their fortunes. Each pig built a house for himself. The first little pig built a flimsy house of straw. The second little pig built an even worse house of sticks. But the third little pig, using more resources and time, built a strong house of bricks. Along came a talking wolf, who implored the first little pig to let him in to his straw house. Sensing danger, the pig said, "Not by the hair on my chinny chin chin." The wolf replied, "Then I'll huff, and I'll puff, and I'll blow your house in." The flimsy house was easily breached by the wolf, who of course promptly ate the pig. The same scenario was repeated with little pig number two. When the wolf, still hungry, encountered the brick house of the third little pig, however, he found a well-built house resistant to his methods. Inside, the third pig was thoroughly prepared for trouble and had a hot cauldron boiling in the fireplace. Meanwhile, the wolf devised a new way to gain entrance, namely climb down the chimney. He thereby slipped and fell into the cauldron, where he was burned to death.

The lesson here is clear. Be thoughtful, resourceful, and above all not lazy. But is being eaten alive and burning a wolf to death the best way to get this across?

Little Red Riding Hood (Le Petite Chaperon Rouge)

This fairy tale dates to the seventeenth century and was written by Charles Perraultt, a French author and intellectual.

Little Red Riding Hood was so named for the colorful red cape and hat that she wore. Upon instructions from her mother, she was allowed to venture out into the woods to deliver food and drink to her sickly grandmother. Grandmother lived deep in the woods, and Little Red was told to stay on the path and avoid strangers. One day, while on a mission to her grandmother, she encountered a talking wolf and foolishly divulged her mission and destination. The big bad wolf ran ahead and entered the grandmother's house, where he swallowed the grandmother whole. The wolf then put on the grandmother's clothes, hopped into her bed, and waited. Soon Little Red entered, only to find a strange-looking grandmother. "What a deep voice you have," she commented.

"The better to greet you with," replied the wolf.

"Goodness, what big eyes you have," Little Red observed.

"The better to see you with," said wolf.

"And what big hands you have," continued Red.

"The better to grab and hug you with," countered the wolf.

"What a big mouth you have," Red stammered.

"The better to eat you with," wolf exclaimed as he jumped out of bed.

The always hungry big bad wolf thereby ate Little Red whole.

The original tale ended here. But in an apparent attempt to soften the horrible impact of this story, an addition was made. This addition called for a hunter to come upon the cabin, seize the stuffed wolf, slit the wolf open with his hunter's knife, whereupon both grandmother and Little Red jump out of the wolf still alive. Whether this disturbing new ending made things better or not I will leave to you to decide.

The lesson here is also clear. Value the safety of the village and avoid the dangers of the forest. Also, beware of strangers and do not speak to them in any detail. An unfortunate by-product of the story, however, is that in this case, the reward for a good deed was to be eaten alive.

Standing above all the other authors and storytellers of fairy tales, both in quantity and pure horror, are the aptly named Brothers Grimm. Jacob and Wilhelm Grimm were nineteenth-century German academics and authors. They wrote many fairy tales, each with a unique and unpalatable subject. Among these were the following, listed with their plot features:

Rapunzel: Child abandonment, false imprisonment

Sleeping Beauty: Curses, death by vipers

Snow White and the Seven Dwarfs: Maternal perinatal death, poison food, dwarfism, glass coffin, death by hot irons

Cinderella: Child slavery, abuse and torture, bullying

The Goose Girl: Talking severed animal head, dragging to death by horses

But perhaps the granddaddy of them all is the tale called *Hansel and Gretel*. This story has something for everyone, including: child abandonment, child servitude, desecration of the dead, false imprisonment, cannibalism, and cremation of a living human.

Hansel and Gretel

This German fairy tale was written in 1812 by the Brothers Grimm.

A great famine descended upon the land, and the cruel stepmother of Hansel and Gretel proposed to the children's father that because they ate too much, they should be taken deep into the forest and abandoned. Reluctantly, the father agreed. Having overheard the conversation, Hansel dropped white pebbles as they were led into the forest. The next day, the brother and sister followed this trail of pebbles back home. The cruel stepmother was furious and forced her husband to take Hansel and Gretel even deeper into the woods and leave them. This time they were truly lost.

After days, they came across a gingerbread house with sugar pane windows. They were famished and began nibbling on the house. Suddenly an old lady came out of the front door and invited them in for food and a nice soft bed to rest. The following morning, the children were surprised to have become prisoners of this evil woman, who turned out to be a witch. The witch practiced cannibalism, and it was clear that she intended to eat at least Hansel. She imprisoned Hansel in an iron cage to fatten him up. Gretel became her slave. Every day, the witch visited the iron cage and asked to feel Hansel's finger as an indication of weight gain. Hansel, seeing that the woman had poor eyesight, substituted a human finger bone that he found in the cage, undoubtedly part of the remains of a previous victim. The persistently thin finger did not deter the witch, who after a few weeks was ravenous for a human meal. She had Gretel prepare the wood-fired oven for the cooking of Hansel. The witch was now so hungry that she decided she wanted to eat both children.

The witch asked Gretel to stick her head into the open oven to test the heat, planning to shove her in while she was in that position. Gretel, sensing a trick, feigned ignorance of what to do. The impatient witch told Gretel to watch and do what she would demonstrate. As the witch bent over and stuck her head into the oven, Gretel pushed her in, slammed the oven door, and bolted it tight. The witch was heard to scream in agonizing pain until she finally died by cremation.

Hansel and Gretel found their way home, only to learn that their cruel stepmother had mysteriously died. The remorseful father welcomed them back.

Well, here is at last a case where the kids win. While a gruesome story, good triumphs over evil, and it is the children's resourcefulness and quick wits that win the day. Unfortunately, a by-product of this story is the lack of parental love and trust. To be taken deep into the woods by a father at a stepmother's urging and to be left there alone is a frightening thought. This act is going to leave a pretty bad taste in the mouth of a modern kid.

So why is there a centuries-old tradition of scaring little children? Is this really a good way to prepare children for some of the inevitable difficulties in life? It's true that there are unexpected risks, bad people, and vicious animals, and children need to be on their toes to deal with these evils. Scaring children may be defended as a means of offering life lessons. Can we buy this? Are these unpleasant and disturbing fairy tales the only way to ensure that important lessons stick?

My wife, as usual, has simplified the answer. She sees no redeeming consequences in scaring children and doesn't look at the old fairy tales as a source of important lessons. It is her opinion that in my case, as she told me, "You just want to show off and exert your power over these little kids."

I have to admit that this bullying and self-gratification theory may hold some water. But do I need this power rush? Am I willing to disturb my grandchildren in order to feel good? I am not ready to accept this as a conscious decision. Unconscious … well, it is possible. In retrospect, as I think about my telling the kids scary things, I do enjoy it. I don't plan these episodes in advance. There is a spontaneity that belies a need to show off and exert power. However, I do not worry about the what-am -I-doing aspect of scaring them.

What of history? Were the creators of clowns and fairy tales actually sadistic bullies? Or were these just misguided or mean-spirited souls who didn't particularly respect children and used the title of author and academic to tinker with the minds of others? In the case of clowns, I am going to give the creators the benefit of the doubt. I suspect that making humans look funny and painting outsized smiles on their faces was predicted to make children laugh. It just backfired.

In the case of fairy tales, I suspect more sinister motives. We can read nationalistic themes in many of these tales, and in the case of Hansel and Gretel, we see, perhaps, the first use of a German crematorium. I think that a take-it-or-leave-it attitude on the part of the Grimm Brothers led them to impart important lessons to the young via the medium of violent fairy tales. However, I have no empirical evidence that useful lessons were ever taught by this means. In my own case, all I can recall about my childhood exposure to these stories is an uneasiness. In fact, the most memorable part of reading those books is the illustrations of ogres and witches. Truly frightening.

So, Emily, I apologize. I have learned a cautionary lesson. While I have come to understand the reasons that I might feel comfortable scaring you, I also realize the price to be paid may not warrant my behavior.

My Love Affair

"You've got to know when to hold 'em, know when to fold 'em, know when to walk away."—Kenny Rogers, "The Gambler"

I Should Have Seen It Coming

I have been having a love affair for the past seventeen years. The object of my affection is a 1997 black Mercedes Benz, model E320. I bought the car upon the occasion of my first promotion to vice president of a large company. One of the perks for the VPs was a generous monthly subsidy for a car of your choice. I developed a tremendous attachment to the car over the years and lavished it with service every 7,500 miles. Despite having been driven 214,000 miles, the car runs like a top. I have replaced any worn-out part, no matter how small or nonessential. In short, the car is in mint condition, or at least it was until recently.

When do you walk away from such an attachment? I guess I told myself that I would know it was time when a major problem developed; a problem so annoying or expensive to fix that I would finally end my relationship. About two months ago, I was unable to start the car at a remote location. Roadside service deemed it worthy of a tow, and a flatbed tow truck was dispatched. The wait for the tow truck was over two hours, which was indeed annoying. On the ride to the dealership for repair, I learned about flatbed tow trucks versus wheel-lift and sling-lift tow trucks. That was the only useful thing that happened that day.

After a week at the service department, nothing could be found. My contact there was Mike, and he said, "The car has started for me every day. Why don't you take the car, and if something pops up then bring it back?"

About a week later, something popped up. The car died while I was driving it, but I was able to get it over to the shoulder of the highway safely. I sat on the roadside, and after thirty minutes, I was able to get it started. I decided that if luck was with me, I could drive the car to the dealer and have the service people start another round of diagnosis. Luck was not with me. The car died again, this time while driving in the right-hand lane of the Caldecott Tunnel, about halfway through the bore. There are no shoulders inside the tunnel, so I was stalled in one of the two active lanes. I was slowing rush hour traffic. I could just hear it in my head, "Stall in the right-hand lane of the Caldecott Tunnel causing major backup of eastbound traffic." Someone even had the gall to honk at me. This time, my call to AAA resulted in the California Highway Patrol being summoned. I was pushed out of the tunnel by the patrol car and told by the officer to call a tow truck. The service people quickly found that my fuel pump had given out. Why this didn't show up on the first visit, who knows. One thousand dollars later, I was back on the road. But had I reached my decision point for getting rid of the car? Was this the problem I had been waiting for? Was this a problem so annoying and expensive to fix that I should walk away? While pondering this question over the next few days, another clue to the answer presented itself.

Bump.

I was driving to work in stop-and-go traffic, when I suddenly felt a hard bump from the rear. I looked in the rearview mirror, and all I could see was a huge truck grill. I leaned out and motioned the driver of the truck to pull over to the shoulder. Upon inspection, my worst fear was confirmed. My rear bumper had a major dent with a hole in the middle. You could actually see inside the bumper. Did you know that there is Styrofoam filling inside a Mercedes bumper? Also, the left rear lights were broken, and the trunk lid was bent up in a bow. The truck had no damage.

The driver, who was wearing a bluetooth earpiece, jumped down onto the ground and looked startled. "What happened?" I asked.

"I don't know," he replied.

After we exchanged names, addresses, contact information, and insurance policy numbers, he added "My name is Fariborz Motalei, but just call me Mike. I can get this fixed without going through insurance," he reassured me. "I know some body repair people through the used car lot I own in Tracy."

Tracy is a small city located about seventy miles away. "That doesn't sound very convenient," I said in a firm voice.

He shrugged and said it was up to me. Given that a rear-ender is clearly the fault of the rear-ender, I quickly decided we would settle this with insurance, his insurance.

After numerous calls, his insurance company said they would accept liability. However, the adjuster had determined that the cost to fix my car would exceed the fair market value of my car. This would result in declaring my beloved car a total loss. Furthermore, the insurance person stated that in this situation, they were obligated by law to report my total loss status to the Department of Motor Vehicles (DMV), and the DMV in turn was going to need to change my title to something called a *salvage title*.

My first reaction was of indignation. *Total loss* and *salvage* were terms that I could not connect in my mind with my car. Here was something I loved and that had treated me so well for so long. The world was spinning, and I didn't know what to do. The insurance person seemed to sense my quandary and tried to be helpful.

"If you don't want to go through all of this," the insurance person said, "we will give you a check for the fair market value of the car. All you need to do is sign the car over to us."

You can sign it over to us! "Oh, my God, what a sad way to part," I thought. Where would they take the car? What would happen to it? They did offer me compensation minus the salvage value if I wanted to keep the car, but in that case I would need to proceed on to the DMV and pass several inspections and get the new salvage title. I found myself getting a bit defensive and feisty. I decided it still wasn't time to walk away … at least not when my car was being called salvage.

The DMV

I knew this was going to be a pretty big deal. The information I received on the phone with DMV suggested that if I completed a brake and lamp inspection, passed a VIN (vehicle identification number) inspection, filled out the paperwork, and brought in my old plates and original title, that I could get the salvage title and new plates on a single visit to the DMV. My mood lightened. Maybe this wouldn't be so bad after all.

Before proceeding, I had an estimate of how much it would actually cost to repair the car. The estimate (best case) was almost five thousand dollars, and the fair (very fair) market value of the car was about thirty-eight hundred dollars. "We almost always find additional damage when we open her up. We can't be sure about things like bent frames from just looking at the car," explained the body shop estimator. "Why would you even consider putting that much money into a seventeen-year-old car with two hundred and fourteen thousand miles?"

That of course was a tough question for me.

My wife kindly took the car for a brake and lamp inspection, and it passed with flying colors. I had just had a thousand-dollar brake job done a few months ago. She gave me the receipt from the inspection, and I loaded it into my accident folder. I was ready for the DMV.

I arrived on a beautiful sunny morning, coming early so that I could remove the license plates. These would need to be surrendered and replaced with new plates accompanying my new salvage title. Upon reaching the check-in desk, I was given three long forms to fill out and told I needed to bring my car around and park in the inspection area in back. This was for the VIN inspection. It turns out that certain shady characters have been known to alter VIN numbers, especially on stolen cars. The VIN inspection is done to make sure that the VIN number displayed on the car still match that on the title. Of interest, there turn out to be several spots where VIN numbers are displayed, including the inside door panel, also on the dashboard, inconveniently squeezed between the window and the part of the dashboard that dives down where the window meets the dashboard, and finally on the engine itself.

I pulled around for the VIN inspection and was joined soon by a DMV official who said that he needed to see my mileage and that I would need to open my hood. The mileage was easy, but for some reason, I couldn't locate the lever that would release the hood latch. I asked him if he knew how to open the hood, and he pointed out that this was my car and that I should have a manual. By then, he had located another problem. A parking lot ticket had fallen down in the front of my dashboard and was wedged between the window and dashboard. It was partially obscuring the VIN number located in this position. I would need to figure out how to remove this. We agreed that it would be best if I just pulled out of his area and didn't come back until I had my act together. After about fifteen minutes, I was back and did pass the VIN inspection.

So far, so good. Still on track for a single visit. Back inside the DMV, however, more problems cropped up at service Window 11. I didn't realize that some of the forms I needed to complete that day included spots for my wife to enter her driver's license number and signature. I was told that if I wanted to drive home, get this done and come back, I could have a one-day pass allowing me to cut the line and get finished that day. Unfortunately, my wife was on an all-day bus tour visiting artists and museums. Strike one. Then I was asked to produce my brake and lamp inspection paperwork. I gave the agent the paper that my wife had given me after she had had the inspection done. "That's not what I need; that's just the receipt," said the clerk.

I explained that was all I had, and we decided that the official white certificates I needed were not in my possession. Apparently, they had not been given to my wife along with the receipt. Strike two.

Finally, I was told that I needed to discuss with my wife whether she wanted her name on the new salvage title. Strike three.

After leaving the DMV, I found out later that the brake and lamp inspection certificates were in the glove box of my car. My wife had placed them there assuming I would need some of the other papers located in the glove box and that I would find these certificates when going through the other papers. I didn't need any of those papers. I would live to see another day at the DMV.

My new appointment for the DMV was set for two weeks after the first visit. I told my wife that she need not come with me, but given the unpredictable nature of the process, I told her to stay on call. No bus tours to occur on this day. As I pulled into the DMV parking lot, I noted the beautiful sunny morning weather, exactly as it was on my first visit. No predicting outcome based on that. As before, I removed my license plates in order to surrender them, as I had hoped to do two weeks earlier. Inside, my number was called quickly, "Serving A005 at Window 1."

As I approached Window 1, I noted that my clerk had dreadlocks and looked preoccupied. I was nervous. From there on, the process was as smooth as silk. All the paperwork was in order, and I surrendered the old plates and was given new plates. I would receive my new salvage title in the mail in two weeks. Suddenly it was over. I went back to my car and began affixing the new plates. As I turned the screws, I began to wonder if this was really the end. As I drove back to work, I noted the smooth and confident performance of my car. Perhaps I could just get a new bumper and not fix the other damage. After all, it was just the bumper that looked so bad. Was it really time to fold 'em, time to walk away?

The Intervention

Not more than a month later, as I was driving down the road, fate intervened again. My wife had told me many times not to follow trucks carrying odd loads. Sure enough, as I followed an old flatbed truck loaded with Sheetrock insulation, it happened. I was traveling at a good clip on the freeway, and traffic was heavy. The first sheet of insulation flew off the truck and up into the air. It flew right over my car. The rest of the load did not. I couldn't stop in time, nor would it have been safe to try, given the close proximity of the car on my rear. "Well, perhaps this is just harmless, lightweight insulation," I thought to myself as I drove directly over several sheets.

As I pulled into my driveway about fifteen minutes later, I noticed that the temperature indicator showed that the car was overheating. I jumped out and saw a puddle rapidly forming on the driveway under my car. I put my finger in the fluid, and it was not oil … it was water.

"We can fix the holes in the radiator," my service advisor, John, told me.

"Please try to do this as cheaply as possible," I requested.

"Well, we can use secondhand parts and get you back on the road for under a thousand dollars," was the estimate.

My wife mumbled something about a money pit when I told her I would be without the car for a week.

Sure enough, about a week later, I was able to retrieve my car. Unfortunately, soon after parking in the driveway, I again noticed a puddle forming under the car. And yes … it was water.

Many apologies and another week later, I finally had the car home and leak free.

Ironically, it was now time to take the car in for its regular service. This was a dreaded event in my house, as it routinely resulted in the need for replacement of expensive, worn-out parts. I asked my wife to pick up the car for me once the service was done, and for the first time, she asked if we could go together. Upon arrival at the dealership, I could see that my service advisor, John, was waiting for us.

"Dr. Pennington," he started, "you need about five thousand dollars' worth of repairs and replacements to keep this car driving safely. The fair market value of the car is about five hundred dollars. What would you like to do?"

I saw that my wife was sitting on the edge of her seat. "Jim, John and I think it is time for a change," she said in a quiet but firm voice. John shook his head in agreement.

It was indeed time to walk away. Within a week, I had ordered a new car. The trade-in I received for my old car was two hundred dollars.

Throwing Things Away

"The truth will set you free …"—John 8:32

The wake-up call was the other day when I noticed several used pieces of dental floss by my bathroom sink. My first thought was "Wow, am I that cheap that I cannot even dispose of disposable dental floss?" As I reused a piece, I pondered what the fair market value of a five-inch-long piece of used medium-grade dental floss might be. I quickly realized that it was less than zero. No, this was not a cost-saving measure; it was something else.

As I get older, I've noticed difficulty in throwing things away. I don't just mean disposable items; rather, many things that might still be useful but to the objective eye are wearing out. I've not observed this trait in my wife or in close older friends. For example, I just threw out a shirt I have been wearing regularly for about five years. The experience should have been relief: good riddance, that is the proper thing an executive should do, and why did you wait so long? But two years ago, when the left cuff started to fray I said, of course, I wear a watch on that wrist. It is the watch that is the culprit, not the shirt. This is the natural order of things, and I forgave the shirt. Now both cuffs are wildly frayed, a seam is opening along the button line, and there's probably some aging I don't even notice. I considered keeping the shirt and always wearing a sweater over it. I even asked my wife for a second opinion, although I knew the predictable response. "Why is a person like you even ask about keeping this shirt?"

As I thought about her question, I realized that I simply didn't consider fraying as a fatal flaw for any piece of clothing. I looked down at my khaki pants and saw that both cuffs were wildly frayed. Furthermore, I had just noted a few days ago that a hole was forming in one leg from wear. My wife had called attention to this new hole and opined that it might be the straw that breaks the camel's back for these pants. "Au contraire," I said, "haven't you noticed that many stylish people are buying their pants with prefrayed cuffs and holes carefully tailored into the legs at strategic positions?"

Granted, I had created this fashion statement the old-fashioned way, by wearing the pants for a long time. But this shouldn't negate the hipness factor that I was trying to push. My wife just rolled her eyes and walked away.

After I noticed the dental floss, I began an inventory of sorts, cataloguing what was clearly a personal syndrome of saving things that might still be of use but not many people would keep around. My cell phone rang, and as I answered it, I realized it was one of the earliest models of smartphones. I purchased my Droid Pro about five years ago. It was my attempt to keep a tactile keyboard yet gain the touch-screen features of true smart phones. Since I bought the phone, Android and Apple have introduced models that are much faster, clearer, and versatile, which makes me admittedly a bit embarrassed to use my phone in public.

I thought about some of my reasons for sticking with this phone. My network, Verizon, doesn't cover Apple ... the original excuse, not valid for several years. I don't want to take the time to learn a new Apple format ... also no longer valid, since I have an iPad now and can make it work just fine. The phone still works ... well, that must be it, but why?

Just as I finished this mental exercise, my other cell phone rang. This phone is a really old Motorola Razor. The phone is tiny and the screen so cracked you can no longer see who is calling. But it is so lightweight and always raises comments when I use it: "Isn't that cute" or "How long have you had that?" I can't bring myself to throw it away. It is part of me. It was in my pocket for twenty-five years. Why would I throw this away just because people make fun of it and me? I'm sticking up for my phone and myself. The phone functioned and still functions perfectly and has advantages that some people have forgotten about. A lot of advancements are not progress but simply change.

I don't know the expected useful life of a modern computer. I imagine eight or nine years might be on the long side. My home computer was at nine years experiencing some boot-up problems, like taking ten to fifteen minutes to get online. It was still working when I did get on, so what's the hurry, I thought? However, when my computer began dropping websites and projects prematurely, I needed to consider a replacement. By now you know: easier said than done. This computer had become my friend. Doing complex searches, helping me work from home, setting up files … the computer was part of my team. I am always loyal to my team members.

I decided to seek help and found someone on the web called the Computer Maven. He listed phone numbers in all of the major areas of the Bay Area. On the phone, I described the problem, and he said, "No problem."

His affirmative response fed my inner beast as far as not throwing the computer away.

The maven arrived the next day wearing a pretty cool cowboy hat. I am not sure of the connection between being a maven and wearing a cowboy hat, but there might be one. Anyway, Ralph the maven's arrival was like Santa dropping down the chimney on Christmas Eve. He was filled with enthusiasm and beamed with confidence. He gave me a wink and went straight to his work.

I told him that I only had three hours before I must leave and wondered aloud if that would be enough time. He looked somewhat incredulous and said, "More than enough for what I need to do."

I thought great, but how does he know what he needs to do without even looking things over?

He said, "This is a classic example of cramming a hard drive overly full of needless applications. The net effect is to slow things down and cause other problems. I see this all the time."

"Wow, what a good deal this is going to be," I thought. This is the type of know-how one can expect from a maven. I told him that I would stay out of his way but to call me in from the other room if need be. "Oh, I need you alright," he chirped, which for some reason sent a bit of concern through my mind. He said he was going to go into the hard drive and go through each stored application one by one. My job was to identify only those apps that I still used.

This exercise was actually interesting. Swear to God, I did not recall more than 10 percent of the apps he found. It was easy picking to get rid of them since I didn't even know what they were. Finally, he said, "Now let me see how it goes."

I retired to the other room, waiting to hear his final comments and instructions. About thirty minutes went by, and I wondered what mavens do to put the final touch on their masterpieces. When I took a peek into the computer room, I saw a different maven. His face was drawn, he had spread manuals and hard discs on the floor, and worst of all, he still hadn't been able to get on the Internet. I quietly asked how it was going. We had actually used up more than two hours and still were not connected. Was the solution overrated? Could the maven have missed his diagnosis?

"This is my worst fear," he told me.

So far, he had not shared his worst fear.

"It looks like you have a virus."

This seemed preposterous to me. We spend a fair chunk of change each year on viral protection programs, like Norton, so this didn't seem sensible. I told this to the maven, although with some humility in deference to his position.

"Oh, you don't know how these viruses can sneak in under these protections?"

No, I didn't. He said there is a very small period of time between turning on the computer and the time that the antiviral software kicks in. It is through this little time window that the virus can take over.

This was quite unsettling to say the least. "Okay," I said, "what next?"

The maven perked up a bit at that question and said he was searching through his diagnostic and therapeutic tools for just the right way to cure this virus. "Just give me time," he said.

I reminded him that we were now at two and a half hours of our three-hour appointment. Then I left the room. About twenty minutes later the maven called me in. He said he had found the virus and expunged it. "You should be good to go. Sorry it took so long," he said.

With all humility, I couldn't resist saying to him, "Looks like your first assumption was wrong." In my mind, he could easily lose the cowboy hat.

"If this happens again, it means a new computer," he told me as he left.

About two weeks later, it happened again. After I spent fifteen minutes on the phone with maven, doing a few probes that I didn't understand, he gave the computer a benediction and thanked me for the business. My new Dell computer is working just fine.

Throwing things away is usually not a contentious exercise. But on our last ski trip, it became just that. Once a year, my wife and I take a trip to a ski resort. Our routine is that we rent skis and poles at the resort but bring along our own boots. The boots can then be fitted to the bindings on the rental skis and off we go. We do this because ski boots are the weak link for an enjoyable ski vacation. It is really hard to find a comfortable pair of boots, so when you do, by all means you keep them. Thus, our old rear-entry boots could be considered dinosaurs, but they are comfortable. In fact, my boots are over thirty years old and still serving me well.

"We don't allow old rear-entry boots to be fitted to our bindings at this rental shop," said the manager.

The manager was a large young man wearing a name tag that said *Aaron from Laramie, Wyoming.*

For some reason, this really upset me. "I have been getting these boots fitted at rental shops all over the world for many years. What is the problem here?" I said.

Aaron tried to keep his professional boot-fitting demeanor and said that these old boots have a tendency to crack and cause serious accidents. He reached into a bin and pulled out a cracked boot to show us. I could see my wife becoming uncomfortable. However, she was uncomfortable with her boots, not with the confrontation with Aaron. My wife suddenly picked up her boots, walked right over to the nearest trash bin, and threw them away. Meanwhile, I gripped my boots harder and tried to decide what to do next. I could sense that Aaron was beginning to lose patience, "Those boots are older than I am," he said.

I entertained the idea of pretending to leave with my boots, then sneaking around to a different counter and having a lower-level person slip me into bindings. I whispered this to my wife. "Are you nuts?" she said.

Aaron stood six foot four, and we were clearly on his radar screen. As I watched rental boots now being fitted to my rental skis, I pondered the next question. Should I follow in my wife's footsteps and visit the trash bin? Or should I take my old boots out to the rental car in the parking lot and leave them in the trunk for the next trip? Even though it would cost me twenty-five dollars to check my boot bag on the flight home, I decided to take the boots home and try my luck again next year. Aaron's ruling might be an aberration or just bad luck.

About two years ago, my boss turned to me and asked, "When are you going to get rid of that old dog?"

That old dog was my 1997 Mercedes Benz E320. My boss drives four different cars, all nice and all new. I was a bit embarrassed and felt compelled to think fast on my feet. I said I was obsessing over leasing versus buying. I also said I wanted to wait for fall to see what the new models looked like. I wondered about new versus used. My boss shook his head and said, "This really isn't the point," and walked away.

From his comments, I realized that he didn't buy my excuses. He saw no reason why I shouldn't buy a new car.

Two years later, I still drive the 1997 Mercedes Benz E320, which now has 228,000 miles on the speedometer. From a distance, the car looks fine. Inside it is mint, and when driving it is smooth and quiet. Up close, one might notice a deep dent on the trunk, resulting from a rear-end collision, and a fog light that doesn't work due to a different accident. My wife considers this car to be a money pit. However, I have developed a deep affection for the car over the years and parting would really be painful for me. This car was given to me upon a promotion to vice president in a major company. Furthermore, it has faithfully taken me to many wonderful places, including the mountains for skiing and the shore for relaxation. And all this transportation has been done safely and in comfort. This car is like a dear friend.

Shortly after my interaction with my boss, I made a pact with myself that should problems occur with the car that became overly time-consuming, expensive, or even just annoying, I would consider getting rid of it. At first, I began to notice the routine but expensive maintenance items like new tires and new brake pads. But then, things began to escalate. Over the past year, I have experienced two tow jobs due to a faulty starter, a rear-end collision that resulted in enough damage that the insurance company called the car a total loss. I was forced to change my title to salvage category. This reduced the fair market value of my car from a thousand dollars to five hundred dollars. Another accident involved Sheetrock materials flying off a truck driving on the highway just ahead of me. I was unable to avoid driving over the sheets of building materials resulting in serious damage under the engine. That took about three weeks for repair. Oh, by the way, I did need to replace the alternator. So far, I consider all of this to be aging-related and a bit of bad luck. All of this time in the repair shop is fine for me, since I have a back-up car. That car is only sixteen years old. It is my baby.

Since I've become aware of my difficulty with throwing things away, I have to ask myself if I am slipping into a neurotic pattern. Will this difficulty lead to inefficiency and slow me down in life? Will this behavior cause me embarrassment with friends and family and prevent a desired level of gravitas in my profession? Lately, sound bites reverberate in my head, "Why is a person like you … " and "That old dog …" and "Isn't that cute, how long …" and "The next time this happens…… " I recently have been recovering from the flu, and for some reason I do my best thinking while weak and convalescing. A few days ago, the truth about all of this suddenly became quite clear. I know why I have such reluctance to throw these old but useful things away. These things are me.

If I can simply discard my loyal car, for example, how easy is it for me or anyone to casually dismiss me socially or professionally? What would become of my relevance? While I consider myself an efficient and high-functioning person, what is the risk of a flashy CEO discarding me in favor of a hot young prospect? While this truth may not be important to everyone, for better or for worse, it is of utmost importance to me. But of what practical value is this new realization, this new truth? Could I apply this new understanding to address my behavior in a painless and rewarding fashion?

In fact, that is exactly what is happening. With this new understanding, I am beginning to look at life and things differently. Rather than act as a protector at all costs, I now am gaining the confidence to give thanks and appropriate goodbyes to possessions that truly have served me well. The key is respect and love. If they must be disposed of now, I know that they have received the love, loyalty, and respect that they deserve.

"You're Too Late"

I moved to the DC area in 1971 to do some medical research at the National Institutes of Health. My friend Marshall told me that the minute I moved from Boston to Washington, DC, I should rush downtown to a liquor store called ABC Liquor. "There," he said, "resides the greatest collection of older Bordeaux wines at incredible throwback prices."

Marshall had lived in DC himself in the late 1960s and spent most of his free time searching for good wine buys. He said the prices on these wines at ABC hadn't changed since they arrived back in the mid to early 1960s. Since Marshall and I had shared many a great bottle during our medical training days in Boston, I trusted him implicitly in matters such as this.

Within weeks of relocating in DC, I headed over to ABC Liquor. As I approached the shop, my anticipation of loading up on treasured bottles at unheard of prices rose rapidly. I anticipated finding such classified Bordeaux as Lynch-Bages, Pichon Lalande, and even some First Growths, like Margaux, Latour, and Lafite. I could taste them already. I parked the car, stepped gingerly onto the sidewalk out front, and entered what appeared to be an unmanned wine store. The shelves were well stocked, but no one was around. I went about my business seeking out the bargains. Clearly the shop specialized in good wines, and I saw many. But, for some reason, I couldn't locate the bargains I was looking for.

"You're too late, young man." The voice came from the back of the store. It was the voice was of an older man with a slight Yiddish accent.

I peeked around the shelves and aisles and finally found the voice's source behind a jungle of racks and boxes. A grizzled old man with a beard sat on a wooden stool in the back of the store. "I know what you want, and they are gone," he announced in an exasperated tone.

"Wait a minute, you don't know me," I blurted out.

"You want the cheap Bordeaux, don't you?" he said smugly. "I've been waiting for you to arrive so I could deliver the bad news."

"Do you know my friend Marshall Wolf?" I asked.

"He called," said the old man.

It was true. The treasures had all been sold. How could this be? Had I been set up, or had my friend exaggerated? Had he told others who happened to get here before me? In any event, I was clearly too late, and I vowed then and there not to be too late for important opportunities ever again.

"What did you guys do today?" the handsome young waiter asked as we sat down for dinner in an Aspen restaurant.

Our party of six included our hosts, Fred and Shelby, plus our close friends, Andy and Teri, and my wife and me. We had been invited to Aspen to spend a few June days with Fred and Shelby in their time-share condo at the base of the mountain.

"Oh, we climbed the Ute Trail," Fred replied.

Our waiter had a look of surprise—perhaps disbelief—on his face as he eyed our group. "We call that trail the butt-kicker around here. Good Job," he sputtered, still looking amazed—and probably thinking we were too old, and thereby too late, to be tackling this particular trail. Our ages ranged from sixty-eight to seventy-eight years young.

We all understood what he meant. We were still shaky from our day of climbing. I for one was indeed wondering if we weren't, in fact, too late for tackling the Ute Trail. Technically, of course, we weren't too late, since all of us, except for Fred's wife, Shelby, had finished the climb. However, in consideration of what had taken place, some of us were functionally too late.

When we had arrived in Aspen two days earlier, Fred and Shelby had everything planned for us, so that we would be able to experience and enjoy this beautiful place to the fullest. Upon arising the next day, Fred said he had a wonderful plan. "We are going to climb the Ute Trail. Shelby and I have done it before, and you will love it. By the way, Shelby won't be able to join us for the climb," Fred explained.

After breakfast, I went to my room to brush my teeth and glanced through a guide pamphlet entitled *Hikes in Aspen*. The trails were rated from 1.0, the easiest, to 5.0, the most difficult. I noted that the Ute Trail scored a 4.5. Thank God it wasn't 5.0. Then I noticed that there were no 5.0 rated trails. To top it off, neither Diane nor I had brought hiking shoes. Sneakers it would have to be on a 4.5 trail in Aspen, Colorado.

As we gathered at the trailhead, I noticed that Fred wore official-looking hiking boots, as did Andy and Teri. "We can take our time with the trail, as we have nothing else planned for the day," Fred said before we started out.

"How long will the climb take?" I asked. Fred shrugged. "I thought you had done this trail before," I continued.

"Yeah, but that was a long time ago," Fred replied.

The climb began, and it didn't take long before we realized this was going to be a serious trek. The trail was consistently steep and narrow with loose footing. There were more switchbacks than I had ever seen on a hiking trail. Faster hikers frequently asked us to make way, all of whom were no older than forty and sported fancy climbing shoes. Some were also equipped with alpine climbing sticks. I noted that a hole was beginning to form on the inside of my left sneaker. My wife, just ahead of me, kept slipping on the loose surface and falling back toward me. I understood why Shelby had been willing to miss the fun this morning.

I also noted that Fred was staying close to me during the climb. "Jim, would you mind taking my pulse?" he asked after we had been climbing for about an hour.

As a physician, I knew how to do this, as well as what to look for. Fred seemed to be a little out of breath and pale. He was not alone on that score. I took his pulse and told him it seemed fine. We continued to climb. About thirty minutes later, Fred, still right behind me, asked me again if I would take his pulse. This time I suggested that it might be good for us all to take a break. We weren't even close to the top.

After another hour, we reached the top of the trail. We were met at the summit by a beautiful broad field suffused with wildflowers and surrounded by rocky cliffs. We sat down, and Fred again asked me to take his pulse. It was still fine, but Fred was clearly exhausted. He wasn't alone. As we sat together, feeling some triumph over the Ute, a thirty-something young woman came prancing by wearing a big backpack. She stopped, smiled, and said, "Well, I don't blame you for resting before the next part of the climb. I do this every day and don't seem to need to take a break here at the halfway station any longer."

She then trotted off, and we looked at one another. What in the world did she mean? We watched as she disappeared onto another trail, hidden in the rocky cliffs. As we later learned, the Ute continues much farther up the mountain. It did so without us.

It was quiet on the way down. Fred did not ask me to take his pulse at all. I could see that we, as a group, were exhausted and a bit surprised at how difficult this climb had been. I wondered how Fred viewed the climb today compared to the last time he had done it some years ago.

In doing an inventory of my body after the climb, I was disappointed at how out of shape I was. My feet hurt, my back ached, and my chest was burning. Or was I simply too late to be doing this?

A few years ago, I was playing golf with my friend Bill, and just to be pleasant, I asked him how his golf game was. I hadn't played with him for some time. "Not so hot. I am spending too much time on my flying lessons," he said.

I was speechless. We were both in our midsixties and I, for one, had never harbored the least interest in learning to fly. Furthermore, it seemed too late in life to be taking on something like that. Just then, a single-engine Cessna flew right over us. As we looked up, Bill said that he was taking lessons in that very model. "It is really fun but very time-consuming," he noted.

After that, it was just a matter of when, not if. I was suddenly smitten by the notion of learning to fly my own plane. And it appeared that I might not be too late. Bill's enthusiasm, coupled with my desire to take on a new hobby as I moved into my later years, added up to a search for an instructor. Several people referred me to a veteran flying instructor who worked at the West Valley Flying Club located at Palo Alto Airport. I contacted Dave by phone, and he agreed to meet me and chat.

I met Dave for lunch on a beautiful early September day. We sat outdoors on the patio by the airport restaurant. Dave dug into his pasta salad and inquired, "What are some of your questions?"

"Is flying a small plane dangerous?" I asked him.

"There are only two things that can really cause trouble. One is engine failure, but you can usually do a powerless glide to an off-field landing," he replied.

By off-field landing I understood him to mean what most of us might call a crash landing.

"The other problem is fire in the cockpit," he noted. "And there isn't much you can do about that."

Well, I reasoned, every activity is a gamble. I could get hit walking down the street. Why not? I agreed to lessons.

"Today we are going to do three hundred and sixty degree turns and then we will work on some stalls," Dave announced at our first lesson.

I wasn't sure what a stall was, but I didn't like the sound of it. "Can you tell me more about a stall?" I inquired.

"Oh, that is when we pull off the power and then lift the nose of the plane higher and higher until we lose the ability to fly," he explained.

"What next?" I stammered.

"Oh, then you do the stall recovery," he said. "That means as the nose of the plane dips down rapidly toward the ground, you apply full throttle, pull back on the yolk as hard as you can, and try to get the plane back to level flight."

Should a sixty-five-year-old man be attempting to stall a plane? Maybe I was too late after all.

But in a few weeks, believe it or not, I was performing power-off stalls with some skill and without anxiety. I just wish they had a different name for the maneuver.

After a few weeks, Dave told me he needed to leave for jet training, whatever that was. He handed me off to a new instructor, Lisa. She was thorough, supportive, and I felt as confident as possible.

Once I completed four months of training, Lisa told me that it was time for a check ride, when an instructor other than your regular instructor flies with you and observes your skills at certain maneuvers. The point of this is to let you and your instructor know how you perform when flying under some pressure. Different check-ride instructors have different styles, and these instructors are randomly assigned by the flight school.

I met my check-ride instructor, Nick, on a cool, gray day. He was young, husky, and could have passed for a wrestler or football player. As I sat with him prior to our flight, he told me: "I'm in a hurry because I have a haircut appointment. Let's get going."

I was slow at everything in those days, and this seemed to irritate him. "You need to learn to prepare the plane for flight more quickly." After takeoff, he said he had a special place he liked to take students. I thought I noted a smirk when he said this but wasn't sure. "There it is," he said as we flew over some foothills.

I looked down. What he seemed to be pointing out was a farmhouse nestled into the hills, and nearby I saw what looked like a short, narrow, dirt-covered driveway. The driveway was actually a man-made landing strip. It was not on flat ground, rather it slanted from side to side and from end to end. I marveled at the skill it must take to land there.

"Try to put it down," Nick ordered.

I felt a dampness in my pants and hoped that he was joking. "Get as close to a landing position for the strip as you can without actually landing," he said.

This was going to be my test of the day. I circled around in hopes of approximating an approach. As I came back around to what I thought was my original location, I looked down and no longer saw the strip. I circled and descended and circled and descended but I never again laid eyes on this small dirt strip. In fact, I became completely disoriented and needed help to get back to the airport.

After landing, Nick took a long look at me. "My observation with old guys like you is that it takes a long time for things to sink in," he said finally. "However, once you finally get it, it sticks well."

This judgment was not reassuring. While he wasn't really saying I was too late to learn, he was saying it was going to be tough.

My next challenge was landings. Our flying club motto was, "Takeoffs are optional, but landings are mandatory."

After a while, I came to realize that if it weren't for landings, many more people could learn to fly. Landing a small airplane, particularly in heavy winds, is difficult. Other than becoming FAA approved for your private pilot license, the single biggest moment for a student pilot is his or her first solo flight. These planes are expensive, and life is precious, so before an instructor gives the green light for a solo flight, the student needs to show consistent landing competence. One day, as my instructor and I landed and rolled down the runway, she told me to pull over to the side taxiway. I stopped the plane, and she opened the door on her passenger side and got out. She then said, "Okay, go do three solo landings, and I will watch you from here."

My stomach twisted. I didn't realize that it is a tradition for instructors to surprise their students when they think they are ready to solo. But, in fact, I was ready. The solo flight and landings went quite well. I had passed a big hurdle. I was now qualified to fly the plane solo. I wasn't allowed to take passengers yet, however.

It appeared that I was not too late.

The culmination of all this training would be an oral and a flight performance exam with a certified FAA check pilot. Successful completion of this exercise meant that I would receive my private pilot license. Before taking the exam, however, the flight school required a dress rehearsal ride with an instructor other than your own. This was meant to offer reassurance or coaching to the student prior to the real thing.

"Hi, my name is Sergei" the pleasant-appearing man said.

Sergei was a young, somewhat short man, who smiled continuously. His accent was clearly Russian.

"I will be doing your rehearsal flight with you," Sergei continued.

Sergei was full of smiles, which helped me relax. However, after I attempted a maneuver called slow flight, it became very quiet in the plane. I sensed that something was wrong. My power-off stall maneuver went well, as did my steep turns. I flubbed my power-on stall, but that didn't seem to bother Sergei. We landed uneventfully, which is how you always hope to land.

After landing we had a debrief session, during which Sergei told me, "If I was the inspector, I would not be able to pass you."

He then spent some time telling me how different people react to failure on the FAA exam. He claimed that in his experience, women tend to cry. Men get mad or go into denial. Many just give up. I asked, "What did I do wrong?"

"You drifted way too high during slow flight, outside the one hundred feet vertical limits above or below the assigned altitude," he explained.

What really upset me was that I hadn't noticed this and felt unsure of how to fix it.

And then I began to worry. Was I too late to fix it?

Several months of hard work later, I passed my FAA flying exam on the first try. I was not too late to earn my private pilot license, but it had probably been a close call. Over the next five years I flew over 560 hours in the air and performed over 1,200 landings. I finally retired from flying at the age of seventy-one, and my wife, who flew with me frequently, declared me to be a good pilot. She doesn't hand out those comments casually.

So I guess you can say I wasn't too late to fly.

"What's the matter with your eye?" asked my colleague.

I was sitting in a conference room and was intermittently covering one eye and then the other to compare vision. It was clear that the vision in my right eye was not right. My colleague had apparently been watching me and to my surprise noted that something must be wrong.

"Oh, I don't think it is anything serious, but my right eye isn't quite right," I told him.

I had noted that morning during my jog that vision in my right eye seemed a bit blurred but dismissed this as not serious. As the day progressed, however, I noted that an enlarged blind spot was evident in the right field of vision. By the afternoon, I was concerned enough to call my physician to describe what was going on. "Get in here now," he said. "We need to check this out today."

At 4:00 p.m. on a Friday afternoon, I showed up in my internist's office and he looked in my eye. "It looks hazy, but you need an ophthalmologist to do the proper exam," he explained. "I will get you in to see someone this afternoon."

Uh-oh, maybe I was too late this time.

The ophthalmologist had clearly stayed late to see me, and it soon became apparent that this was fortunate. "The pressure in your right eyeball is very high," he said. "I am going to apply some drops now to try to get it down."

"What does this have to do with my blind spot and blurred vision?" I asked nervously.

"Well, when the pressure becomes too high in the eye and stays that way for some time, it will damage the optic nerve. That in turn results in loss of vision. This loss is partial at first, but if left too long, it will progress to blindness," he explained. "This condition is called glaucoma, and it is common. Usually, if one has annual eye checkups, this can be detected at an early stage, and vision can be preserved by regular use of eye drops. How long has it been since you had your eyes examined?" he inquired.

I fidgeted in my chair. Finally, I confessed, "I think it has been three years or more."

I could see that he was surprised and puzzled why someone my age, particularly with a medical background, would go so long without an eye checkup. However, no one was in the mood for lectures. The job at hand was to get the pressure down and stabilize it within in a safe range. He applied some strong eye drops, and within twenty minutes the pressure in the eye had fallen dramatically. "Here, take these drops with you and put two in your right eye twice a day," he instructed. "I want to see you on Monday and see how you are doing."

I was in his office bright and early Monday. His exam showed that while the pressure was clearly down, it wasn't quite where it should be. "We are going to need to add more medicine or do a laser procedure," he said.

"Will this visual loss be permanent, or will I recover some vision as I treat the glaucoma?" I asked.

"Unfortunately, the loss will remain. The objective now is to prevent further loss," he answered.

And so it seems that I had forgotten my vow never to be too late. I had been far too late in having my eyes examined. But I wasn't too late to save the eye.

You're Too Early

My wife and daughter are the ultimate planners. They could be considered uberplanners. They will never be too late for anything.

On July 25, 2015, I received a copy of an e-mail from my daughter sent to my wife. She was inquiring about our availability for a weekend visit on March 11, 2016. Since this was eight months away, I imagined this to be a typo, perhaps inquiring about October or November, later this year. To my surprise, my wife's e-mail response was that we already have tentative plans for that weekend. I then got a call from my wife, who said, "Do you really want to attend Cal Performances on March 11, 2016?" At this point, I was slightly disoriented. I hoped I would be well and happy on March 11, 2016, but I certainly had no idea that plans were actively in play for something that far away. "Well, what is playing at Cal Performances that night?" I responded.

Since we have a tradition of looking ahead at the Cal Performances schedule for the next season, I suspected we had discussed interesting performances. But this would be far ahead of when tickets go on sale.

"Oh, I think it is the Mark Morris Dance Group doing that frog thing," she said.

I guessed that what she meant by the frog thing was the wonderful comic opera by Jean Philippe Rameau called *Platee*, a fantasy about a human-size, ugly but lovable frog. We saw it performed years ago by the Mark Morris Dance Group. My wife considered it to be weird. I loved it. For some reason, whenever she sees Mark Morris scheduled, she thinks it is going to be the frog thing.

I could tell that she had no interest in attending this on March 11, 2016. I looked up the schedule for March 11, 2016, and found that Cal Performances was, in fact, doing a Mark Morris performance, but it was to be *L'Allegro, il Penseroso* by Handel. It would not be the frog thing. However, to help with their planning, I told my wife that I would be happy to skip the evening performance on March 11, 2016. We could now let Cynthia know that we would be available for a visit in eight months' time.

One of the rationales for this advance planning is to obtain the cheapest airfares. Waiting for fares to rise would certainly qualify as being too late.

"Well, are you still up for the tour?" my wife cautiously asked one Sunday as we turned out of the driveway of our golf club. She was at the wheel.

"What tour?" I responded, having no recollection of signing up for a tour.

"The cemetery tour I've been discussing," she said.

"Who died?" I questioned. I began having an uneasy feeling that this cemetery tour had something to do with me.

"No one, this tour is for planning purposes. I know it is not just around the corner, but it will make me feel better to have an idea of what you want. I don't want to deal with this at the last minute," she explained.

"Want for what?" I said, though I now knew where she was going with all this.

On several occasions, my wife had mentioned that she would really like to have an idea of what we both want when we pass away. I avoided much detailed discussion when this topic came up. I thought, or at least hoped, that we had ample time to deal with this. But given that several deaths of people we have known had occurred in the past few months, I knew that my wife was going to insist on getting more granularity around this issue.

I told her I was willing to do the tour but hoped it wouldn't take too long. She was absolutely delighted; it appeared that a great weight was going to be lifted off her back.

Cemetery number one on the tour was located just a few miles from our house, in a lot next to the Lafayette Park Hotel. I didn't catch the name of this place. I had always assumed this was a pet cemetery, but my wife assured me as we turned in that humans were buried in the back. Sure enough, human graves appeared as we ventured further into the place. The ground was brown. I couldn't tell whether it was dried up grass or just dirt. As we turned a bend, we saw a dilapidated shed, badly in need of paint, with loose boards here and there. I assumed the equipment was housed here. Then I noticed a small dirty sign attached to the building, which said Office. "Let's get out of here," we exclaimed in unison.

Next, my wife said we were on our way to Pleasant Hill, a town adjoining our hometown of Lafayette. "There are two cemeteries there that might work," she announced. On the way over, she asked, "Do you remember what I want?"

"Want for what?" I absently responded.

"For my body when I die, of course," she quickly answered. "That's what we are doing today, isn't it?"

"Cremation," I said.

"Yes, but then what?" she asked.

"Well, I think you want to have your ashes spread to the winds," I fortunately recalled. "Would you like me to take you up to the Mendocino Coast and cast you out to sea? I know you love the sea."

"Oh no, I heard about someone trying that who accidently slipped off a cliff and fell to his death as he tried to throw ashes. That is definitely too dangerous," she said emphatically.

"Too bad I don't fly my little plane anymore," I noted. "I could open the window in flight and throw you out."

"Wouldn't the ashes just blow right back in through the window?" she asked.

"Good point. I recall that the window did accidently come open in flight once, and the rush of wind into the plane from outside was terrific," I acknowledged. "I will find a nice, safe place to throw you in the water."

"Okay, just not a lake," she instructed.

We were nearing the next cemetery, and I was straining to find the sign. I saw it, and we turned in.

Cemetery number two was called Queen of Heaven. We drove down a long entrance road before reaching the cemetery proper. "I don't like all this religion," commented my wife.

I didn't know what she was talking about, as we hadn't even reached the cemetery grounds yet. But I could tell that she was already not comfortable with the place. We turned into the burial grounds per se, and I was happy to see green lawn and lots of flowers. "Wow, look at all those plastic flowers. That is a sea of plastic flowers," blurted my wife.

"How do you know they are plastic flowers?"

"Too bright, no brown spots, and nothing falling over," was the impressively analytical response. No more questions, Your Honor.

"Aha, I knew it," said my wife suddenly in a tone of voice suggesting disapproval.

She had spied the sign, indicating that this cemetery was part of the CFCS network, which stood for Catholic Funeral and Cemetery Services. The car was already doing a U-turn, and we headed back to the long entrance road. As we drove back and approached the front gate, curiosity led me to ask how she had known this was going to be too religious before we even got to the burial grounds. "It was that big blue thing. Just look at that," she pointed out.

Standing just inside the entrance gate was a tall cement pillar, upon which was perched a huge blue-clad statue of the Virgin Mary. A gold halo floated above her head. I had been so busy looking for signs as we drove in that I had missed this. My wife sees everything, however.

Cemetery number three was located just a short drive away. This was Oakmont Memorial Park.

It was clear as we drove in that my wife was familiar with this place. I was reminded that our recently deceased friend and neighbor had been cremated here. In fact, my wife recalled that her husband had to leave a lunch with friends early to come over here and pick her up. As we drove around, the mood continued to lighten. "Would you like a view?" my wife inquired.

"A view of what?" I asked.

"Well, I know it might be more expensive, but we could request that your grave would be located on top of one of these rolling hills," she noted.

"Who cares if I am dead?" I mused.

"It might be more cheerful for visitors to have a nice vista—that's all," she opined. "Look, there's the office. I am going in to pick up a map."

We parked behind a large hearse in the parking lot, and I waited in the car. Upon her return, I inquired how it had gone inside. "Well, the man asked if I was planning a service. I told him no, my husband is out in the car."

The tour was coming to an end. We wound our way through the hilly burial grounds, passing small, medium, and in some cases impressively large stone grave markers. At one point we drove by a seven-foot-tall monument with the name of a prominent and well-heeled family printed on the front. I noted that I might look good with that type of marker. My joke did not elicit a response. We exited Oakmont Memorial Park and headed for home. The planning had been a great success, and my wife was in a wonderful mood. "Now that wasn't so bad, was it?" she asked as she patted my knee.

The Bear Button

"You'll know it when you see it."

We had dinner the other night with our friends Steve and Stephanie who had just returned from Alberta. They told us about playing a round of golf at a course in Canmore, and to their surprise there was a large button on their golf cart prominently labeled "Bear Button." As they began their round, their attendant instructed them that should they see, or worse yet, be attacked by a bear, they should push the Bear Button.

I asked what would happen next. They weren't sure because they never pushed the Bear Button. "Well, what do you think would happen?" I asked. And they replied that their impression was that someone, or maybe a bear team, would come out and shoo away the bear.

"How would they do that?" I asked.

They had no idea; they hadn't pushed the Bear Button.

"What kind of bears might be encountered?" I asked.

"Both grizzlies and black bears are common in those parts," they said.

I didn't ask, but I wondered to myself whether I would prefer a grizzly or black bear to be my intruder. I did ask what might happen if multiple bears showed up at the same time at different locations on the golf course, and multiple golfers pushed their bear buttons at the same time. This complex question was well beyond my friends' ability to answer.

Since dinner the other evening, I have spent considerable time thinking about the Bear Button. My wife is puzzled about why I keep bringing it up for conversation. "This is just another example of a warning system, isn't it?" she said. "Isn't this just like a burglar alarm or air-raid siren?"

"No," I told her, "I think the Bear Button may be unique and brings up a few issues for consideration."

First is the paradox of a Bear Button on a golf cart. Golf is a relaxing sport, a chance to enjoy the great outdoors and to do so in a somewhat sophisticated surrounding. I have played golf myself many times over the years, and adding any increment of danger, anxiety, or fear has never been remotely on the table. Being on a golf cart staring at a Bear Button seems to me a big disconnect.

Even more unsettling is that the result of pushing the Bear Button is apparently unknown to the user and perhaps unpredictable. Is there really a threat from bears? Is there really a bear team that will come to the rescue? Is this really just a big joke perpetrated on visitors to Alberta to give them something to tell friends later at dinner? But if that is the case, what purpose does it serve?

Keeping in mind these potential drawbacks, namely that a Bear Button might be unsettling and possibly unreliable, might there also be important positive features of a Bear Button?

Let's say we allow for a Bear Button in our lives. Let's agree that having a nice day, or even nice life, can benefit from a metaphorical Bear Button. Do we have one already, and would it be good to have one if we don't? But then would we even recognize a Bear Button if we possessed it? If so, how? And could we comprehend what would happen if we pushed it?

I, for one, have decided that I would like a Bear Button. I am not sure exactly how to obtain one for daily living, but I believe with careful thought and planning I might figure this out.

It is not hard to imagine some situations where a Bear Button would be useful, but then I have to ask: How important might it be to depend on a Bear Button? And are there acceptable and unacceptable times for pushing your own Bear Button?

Given all these questions regarding a personal Bear Button, it appears that a set of rules for using a Bear Button would be helpful.

Rules for operation and use of a personal Bear Button:

1. Available twenty-four seven

2. Results not controlled by operator

3. Outside forces involved

4. For use in situations of concern or threat

5. For use when quick or urgent action needed

6. Element of uncertainty of effectiveness

To help establish the proper use of a Bear Button, it also would be helpful to determine situations in which a Bear Button might have been of use had one existed.

The Man in the Boxer Shorts

Hotels can be risky places. When one frequents them as often as I did in the days when I traveled for a living, it is only a matter of time. As an academic, I was frequently on the lecture circuit. On a trip from my home in Boston to San Francisco, I arrived at my hotel, the Hyatt Union Square, late in the evening. I was tired and hungry, and even though it was after eleven o'clock, I ordered a sandwich and a beer from room service. Upon finishing, I decided to put the tray in the hallway since I didn't want to smell it all night. I tried an acrobatic maneuver, holding the door open with one foot while leaning forward and reaching out with the tray to place it in the hall. Suddenly I slipped, my foot dropped off the door, and the spring-loaded door swiftly closed, leaving me in the hallway. Unfortunately, I was wearing only a pair of boxer shorts.

It was now close to midnight, and I was on the twenty-third floor. Fortunately, there are not a lot of people milling around the halls at that time of night. I reasoned that I could quickly and discreetly walk out to the elevator area and call security on the house phone, which would most certainly be on the table by the elevators. Upon arrival, I was horrified to find that no such phone existed. Where was the house phone I have seen by elevators in every hotel in which I had ever stayed?

Where was my Bear Button?

Suddenly the elevator opened, revealing a packed-in crowd of people returning from their evening out. I looked at them, and they looked at me. Their eyes opened wide, and I could hear an audible gasp. One couple clearly starting to emerge from the elevator changed their minds and stayed onboard. "Please call security," I yelled as the doors were closing. About twenty anxious minutes later, a security man arrived and let me back into my room.

"Don't worry about it," he said. "This happens all the time."

Water, Water Everywhere.

As part of my academic travels, my wife and I were invited to visit and lecture in Thailand. We were to be guests at a beachside resort about an hour's drive south of Bangkok. Our hotel looked pretty nice as we drove up, but once in our room on the eighth floor, we noted that it was not well built. For example, there was about a two-inch gap between the floor and the bottom of the door to the hall, and the bathroom fixtures were very cheap and loose. In preparation for our banquet dinner, I needed to use the toilet. I couldn't help but notice that the flushing handle for the toilet was connected to a large pipe, which in turn was connected to an even larger pipe emerging from the wall beneath the toilet. I had never seen this type of plumbing before. As I pulled on the flushing handle, things didn't feel right. Suddenly the handle and the entire top section of pipe came off in my hands. Water immediately gushed up through the two-inch hole like a geyser. This was Old Faithful in my bathroom.

My wife heard the commotion and came running in, but stopped in her tracks when she saw the catastrophe. We both said at once, "Let's call Front Desk."

By now water was covering the floor of our entire room and starting to leak out under our door into the hall. Things were moving fast and required quick action to prevent a really big problem. While my wife put our luggage on the bed, I called Front Desk. A message said they were away but would return in due time. "Let's call Engineering," we both said.

My call to Engineering went completely unanswered. I assumed they had minimal staff in the evening hours. By now, water covered a meaningful portion of the eighth floor of the hotel.

Let's find a Bear Button.

Eventually, as water reached a depth of about four inches on the eighth floor and began showing up on lower floors, hotel staff arrived. My wife and I asked that we be moved to a higher floor.

Round and Round She Goes; Where She Stops Nobody Knows

Boating with friends can be fun and usually is … but not always. Several years ago, my wife and I visited our old friends, Russ and Althea, at their summer home on Cape Cod, Massachusetts. These friends have owned a nice inboard motor boat for years, and one of the highlights of a visit is to head out onto Cape Cod for a cruise. We set out from East Denis on a beautiful August afternoon, heading to Provincetown. This would be about a twenty-mile trip across the Cape, but our boat was powerful and would be skippered by the highly regarded Captain Russ. We did need to keep an eye on time, however, since we had a reservation that evening for dinner at 7:00 p.m. at the nicest and most difficult to book restaurant on the Cape.

All went well on the trip over, and we enjoyed walking around Provincetown for several hours. Time was passing, however, and we were already anticipating a great dinner. We climbed back aboard the boat and set our course back to East Denis Harbor. I marveled at the skill of our skipper as he seemed to pick a target on the distant shore and keep our heading true, adjusting for wind and drift. Given that it was a bit later than planned, we were moving along at a pretty good clip.

Suddenly Skipper Russ slowed the boat. I looked up and noticed that our target had moved considerably to the left. "Hey, are we going in circles?" I asked.

Skipper Russ looked concerned. "Yeah, it appears that way. Let me check this out," he said.

After a quick inspection of the rudder, it was confirmed that it was stuck in a position to the right. Furthermore, it was extremely hard to move by hand and impossible to move with the steering wheel. We were destined to go in circles. We were going to miss dinner.

I needed a Bear Button.

Russ informed us that the Coast Guard rarely patrolled this area. Our only hope was for me to lean out over the back end of the boat, grab the rudder, and force it into a position as close to straight as I could. And this must be done continuously until we reached shore. "I don't know if I can do this," I said.

"You better do this, or we are in real trouble," Russ said. "And you can forget about dinner too."

I took my position, we fired up the engine, and we proceeded cautiously. The effect of my effort was to reduce but not eliminate our drift to the right. Somehow, we finally made it to shore, landing a number of miles up the shore from our intended destination in East Denis Harbor. And we missed dinner.

Thinking about the Bear Button, I realized that life is a difficult business at times, and the Bear Button might be used for considerably more serious situations.

The Eyes Have It

I wear glasses. But with correction, I get along fine. Renewing my driver's license has never been a problem due to eyesight.

A few weeks ago, while sitting in a conference room, I was startled by what seemed to be a gray veil drawn down over about 30 percent of my right eye. This apparent sudden loss of vision was frightening, and I ran through the possible causes in my mind. Stroke, bleeding inside the eye, and retinal detachment were all on the list and all bad news.

I wanted to reach for a Bear Button.

A call to my regular doctor resulted in a referral to see an ophthalmologist that day. I had not had my eyes checked for two years so had no clue what might be going on. The eye specialist quickly found the pressure inside my right eye was twice as high as normal. He applied some drops, and within fifteen minutes the pressure was dropping. However, he then said, "I think I see something abnormal going on in the back of your eye. You need to see a retina specialist."

The next day, a retina specialist, who is a specialist of a specialist, said, "I think I see some bleeding in the retina. You need a special exam as soon as possible."

I needed the Bear Button a second time.

All's well that turns out well. At least relatively well. The special exam, done two days later, showed no bleeding in the eye. The final diagnosis was glaucoma in the right eye, which can be treated easily by daily eye drops.

An Unmet Medical Need

I can recall a number of sad and even life-threatening situations where a Bear Button might have been useful. No situation was worse than the illness endured by my younger brother. John had suffered from Hodgkin's Disease when he was in college and was treated successfully with radiation therapy. Twenty years later, he began developing leg weakness upon walking. This progressed and after two more years a new problem developed; he was becoming quite short of breath while walking. A chest x-ray revealed scarring in his lung tissues and fluid around his lungs. A diagnosis of postradiation fibrosis was made. This is a condition occurring years after radiation treatment in which scar tissue begins to form spontaneously in various organs leading to disruption of their normal function. In addition to involving his spinal cord, the cause of his weakness in the legs, his lungs were extensively involved. Eventually, his lungs deteriorated to the point where he needed to be on a ventilator machine. Where was the proper medicine to treat this advancing fibrosis? Where was something to save his life? Despite extensive research no such medicine existed.

Where was the Bear Button?

After these reflections, it became more realistic to understand how a personal Bear Button might be useful. The human mind is inquiring, however, and just at the moment you acquire a personal Bear Button, you are likely to ask what it really is. Is a Bear Button no more than simply luck or fate? Or is a Bear Button religion? My advice is not to try to understand too much about it. You will know when you have one, and you will know when to use it.

My Fall with Mandy

"Doctor, Doctor, it hurts when I walk on my right foot."

Response from doctor: "So don't walk on your right foot."

—Henny Youngman

During the fall of 2011, I spent three hours each Tuesday afternoon attending acting class with Mandy Greene, during which time I alternated among being furious, frustrated, insulted, physically uncomfortable, and freezing cold. "Why do I keep going back each week?" I asked myself. Why did I keep walking on my right foot?

The answer is apparent only in retrospect: I was fascinated by what was going on and learning things I had not known. However, the price I paid was high. As an accomplished academic physician at Harvard Medical School and a successful executive in the pharmaceutical industry for thirty years, why did I allow myself to be made to roll around on a dirty floor for hours and be told my questions were stupid questions?

The Start of a New Life

Given that in the late summer of 2011 I was sixty-nine years old, I had considered answers to the commonly posed question of what I would do when I retire. Well, I had considered many things, including going into the priesthood. I loved to give lectures. I spent many days during my academic career lecturing, both as part of my academic duties as well as during numerous visiting lectureships around the country. And a sermon is just a lecture, isn't it? But I eventually decided against the priesthood. I had concerns that church politics and seniority issues might have me making house calls and teaching Sunday school for a long time before I could mount the pulpit.

How about something in the wine industry? I collected and studied wine for over forty years, so this was a logical choice. But I was concerned about getting caught doing backroom business, such as inventory or negotiating prices, instead of more glamorous marketing and sales activities. Working in a restaurant as the wine advisor also appealed to me. But wouldn't the appearance of a sixty-nine-year-old sommelier tableside at a fine restaurant be unexpected and perhaps unwelcome?

How about acting? I had always wondered what secret sauce actors had obtained to be able to do what they do. I felt confident in my creative side, my ability to imagine and express. In fact, I considered myself a natural. After all, hadn't I spent a major part of my career on lecterns and making videos putting messages across? I saw actors immersing themselves in parts, using their emotional experiences to develop their characters, which was something I appreciated and could do. I admired performances such as Al Pacino in *Danny Collins*, a complex aging man, Tom Hanks in recent roles, such as Captain Phillips, and even the older Marlon Brando as the godfather. Yes, this was for me.

In August 2011, our little biopharmaceutical company had a severe financial setback. In my role of advisor and senior statesman, I was a luxury for a small company in financial trouble. I was laid off, which meant that "what are you going to do when you retire" … was now. The good news was I had time and freedom of schedule to pursue interests that might require daytime weekday hours. While I still consulted with my company and was in the office for several hours most days, I was able to start a new life. I decided that I would explore acting.

I am not one to go halfway on projects. I want to tackle the most complex assignment, the most esoteric art, the most exotic food. While at the time I really didn't know much about method acting, I did know that this was considered the highest form of the profession and that most of the great contemporary actors and actresses, like James Dean, Marilyn Monroe, Marlon Brando, Jack Nicholson, Al Pacino, Dustin Hoffman, and many other great artists convincing and successful in their craft had trained in the method. I wanted to join the club. Rather than study articles, books, and seek out experts to better understand what I was going to be getting into, I opened up the computer and searched for method acting schools. This was not the most thorough or careful approach, but it turns out it led to a most interesting experience.

Method Acting

Until the late nineteenth century, the traditional method for teaching the craft of acting was imitation of established actors. The actors in turn decided how they wanted to play the part, regardless of what the playwright may have intended. This led to a predictable and stiff style of acting that did not permit much creativity or expression of deep emotions. Constantine Stanislavski (1863–1938), the father of method acting, was born in Moscow to wealth, thus with time to pursue artistic endeavors. He focused on acting and directing. After a brief stint in a traditional acting school, he decided to explore new directions. At the Maly Theater, he found a style of acting called psychological realism, a new method to develop actors of feeling. The actor became the character and identified with his or her thoughts and feelings; he or she would walk, talk, think, feel, cry, or laugh as the author wanted him or her to do. Stanislavski built this concept into a true method based on two concepts. One was called emotion memory, in which the actor used his or her own past emotional memory of personal events to project into the acting of the role. The other concept was the method of physical actions, in which the actor uses sounds and motions to release subjective emotions and feelings.

In the United States, the most famous proponent of method acting was Lee Strasberg, who along with several colleagues started the Group Theater in New York in 1938 and began teaching the method based on Stanislavski's teachings. Strasberg stressed more of the psychological and less of the physical methods. In 1951, he founded Actors Studio in New York, and later he founded the Lee Strasberg Theater and Film Institute in New York and Hollywood. The American actors who studied with Strasberg read like a who's who of acting. What appealed to me was the way critics described method actors: "They communicate emotions they really feel; summon emotions from their own life to illustrate a stage role; act from the inside out." This did not intimidate me but rather further convinced me that I could do this.

Mandy

As I looked over the numerous Bay Area acting schools advertised on the Internet, I focused on schools promoting method acting. Why beat around the bush with amateur approaches when I could go for the real deal? The Workshop for Actors, whose founder and lead teacher was Mandy Greene, jumped out at me. Mandy had a résumé that included time with Lee Strasberg at Actors Studio in New York, and she had several endorsements by famous actors. The photographs of Mandy on the website depicted a rather young-looking woman, but given her résumé, including a long period in Spain in the 1980s, it seemed to me that she would actually be closer to my age. But age didn't matter, for as one actor said in his endorsement, "Mandy is the real deal."

I decided to go with The Workshop for Actors. Had I taken the trouble to look up the school and Mandy on Yelp, I would have found a different description of Mandy: "an old, cooky [sic] woman, condescending, destructive."

To say that Mandy Greene is a complex person does not do her justice. The list of adjectives referring to her is long and highly varied, depending on the observer. In this case, I am the observer. First of all, Mandy was indeed older than her photos on the web. She appeared to me to be in her midsixties, but this may be generous. She was best described as a stylish hippy—big hair, big glasses, big sweaters, and big jewelry. In contrast, she drove a really small car and had a small dog.

Since the front door of the building that houses her studio was always locked and stayed that way until she arrived, we students would congregate out front on the sidewalk and watch her arrival in the small car each week. It is uncanny how there was always an open parking space for her right across the street from the front door. Her dog in her arms, she would walk over, smile, and unlock the door. There was a sense of presence about her, and she knew it.

The line between arrogance and confidence is thin, and Mandy displayed both. One day, out of nowhere she announced, "What a great feeling I had in the coffee shop today on my way to class. I basked in the knowledge that I am a world-class drama teacher heading off to give of myself to my students."

She indeed was carrying a cup of takeout coffee, which she nursed for over an hour.

Without question, Mandy displayed a consistent and strong vision of the artist. This was her most valuable teaching skill. She made sure that everyone was clear that her goal was to help us understand what it takes and means to be an artist as an actor. "Simply doing karaoke acting is not enough," she would stress.

She used the pyramid as a tool to make her point. Pulling out her laptop computer, she would boot up the pyramid lesson. At the base of the pyramid were our basic needs to live: food, air, water, and sleep. On the next level was our need for love, warmth, understanding, and communication with our fellow humans. The next level up was our intellectual self. Here we perform in our job, profession, or trade and display the fruits of our schooling and hard work. Finally, we reached the peak of the pyramid. This is where the artist lives, a level for dreamers, visionaries, and creators. Mandy was quick to point out that not everyone could achieve this highest level, but that is where she hoped to lead us. It was clear that she lived here. The anatomical location of this pyramid peak is the right brain. True artists express right brain function well, and we must work on doing this. As a physician, I was interested in this concept. I tried hard to remember any such training about the right brain during medical school. I came up blank.

The Studio

Years ago I learned that *form* and *function* work together. The *form* for our venue for instruction was not ideal for optimal *function*. In fact, I cannot imagine a less commodious studio than the one Mandy rented for her classes. The location was on a small, dark, side street in the Mission District of San Francisco. The building was on a block filled with denizens who were either dirty or scary or both. Was it dangerous to park on this block and attend a three-hour class? I never felt it to be, but I could have been fooling myself.

The building housing our studio was a nondescript multistory structure in the middle of the block. An iron gate, always locked, guarded the door. We found no use for the intercom by the entrance. Once Mandy arrived, we entered and ascended several flights of dimly lit stairs to her studio. This was a barren room with wooden walls, also dimly lit, with a stage on one side and forty feet across the room from the stage a tiered deck for chairs. A filthy, dark, matted rug covered the floor between the stage and the tiered deck. I doubt that janitorial services were included in the rent. A few photographs of actors hung on the wall. As for the temperature, that pretty much mimicked the outside temperature. The room was warm when I started classes in late August. By October I began noticing that my toes and nose were unusually cold during the sessions. By November, there were days when I shivered from the cold. Floor exercises were particularly unpleasant. I looked around for a source of heat, but to no avail. Realizing that there was no heat provided in the studio, I began wearing heavier and heavier clothing to class. By December, ski parkas were the norm.

The Process

When I signed up for the classes, they were offered in blocks of eight or sixteen weekly three-hour sessions. I asked Mandy when the curriculum would begin so that I could start with the rest of the class. She explained that was not how the system worked. "My classes are like a moving train. You can get on and off whenever you want."

Of course, that is not in the comfort zone for a well-organized person used to carefully planned and executed learning experiences. That should have been a warning to me that Mandy's approach and my approach were going to clash. In fact, they systemically clashed, which undoubtedly slowed my progress. That was not a fault of either party, just a fact. Mandy sensed this problem too. "Are you serious about acting or just along for the ride?" she asked me.

By now, you probably will be surprised to learn that we actually did have the semblance of a daily class routine. A typical class would be about three hours long. It always began with a Mandy-chat. Then, we would move on to exercises, and finally individuals would perform preassigned pieces. The chat was generally about thirty minutes long and invariably included negative comments about men and nonartists. Strangely I actually found these chats fascinating. I had never experienced such uninhibited and unapologetic bias and vitriol. During these chats, most of the talking was one way. Mandy generally met any of my attempts to ask a question with "That's a stupid question," or "I'm not a psychologist, I am an artist." There is an old saying that "there is no stupid question," but Mandy never ascribed to that aphorism.

The exercises were either floor exercises or chair-on-the-stage exercises. Although I didn't realize it at the time, these exercises were classical, resembling those taught by Stanislavski in his method of physical action. We would lie on our backs on the floor and let our legs flop down from a cocked position flat onto the floor. This was surprisingly hard, especially as you tried to figure out how dirty the floor really was. On the stage, we were to sit in a chair and let our bodies, arms, and legs become limp. Mandy encouraged us to let out screeches or groans to accompany movements. Mandy insisted that my noises were too loud, not loud enough, too nasal, or just plain wrong. It was amazing how many wrong ways I found to make noises.

Another exercise was classic emotion memory. Since I didn't consider outside homework important, I didn't understand how important this exercise was. For me, the most effective assignment was to picture yourself in a room from childhood and conjure up the feelings you experienced in the room. Having had a really colorful and difficult childhood, this led to my experiencing many strong feelings: everything from sadness and anger at my father, pity for my mother, and general disappointment with my family situation. Later, I prepared a scripted skit based on these feelings. When I asked Mandy if I could perform this for the class, she said it was scripted and didn't fit the format of our exercise ... permission denied! I later performed the skit for my wife at home, and she cried for two days. I was learning method acting despite Mandy.

Mandy dedicated the final hour of the class to her favorite students, those females who had been in class a long time. One woman did frequent bits that always ended with uncontrolled sobbing. Her conversation on the phone about what happened last night (she was raped) with her boyfriend was a classic. I called her the crier, and I always felt uncomfortable when she got up to perform. In my eyes, she was a ham rather than an actor. Another very large woman was there to enhance her operatic performances with more emotion. Her arias were startling in this small room. "I am here to spite my father," she explained to the class.

One day, Mandy asked me to do a reading with a young female student of a passage from a play by Henrik Ibsen called *The Master Builder*. I was to read the part of Halvard Solness, an aging architect who was basking in the triumph of a successful career. The other student read the part of Hilda Wangel, age twenty-four, who had apparently been sexually involved with Halvard in days gone by. One day, the girl paid a visit to Solness in his office to confront him with promises he had made to her years ago and which had led to her cooperation with him in those earlier days. The other student and I sat close together as we read script from the same book, our arms pressing together as we strained to read in the dim light. It wasn't long before I felt both an attraction for and a discomfort with Hilda Wangel. I sensed my partner also getting into this. I'm sure these were the feelings that Ibsen intended. When we finished, Mandy, who had been sitting on the edge of her chair with her mouth open said, "That was delicious."

But certain other sessions were not successful for me. My next assignment was to read the part of Shelley "The Machine" Levene from the David Mamet drama *Glengarry Glen Ross*. Jack Lemmon played this role in the movie. Glengarry Glen Ross is the story of four real estate salesmen trying to pedal property in two new housing developments named Glengarry and Glen Ross. Shelley Levene is by far the oldest in the office, and while once a successful salesman, he is now desperate to close a sale. In short, he has become an aging loser under immense pressure to perform or be fired. This part was tough for me. How was I to establish past emotional memories of being an aging loser when I was in fact an aging winner? I tried to fake it by acting stressed, but Mandy wasn't having any of it. She turned and walked away in the middle of my reading. To redeem myself, I asked her, "Can I tell a few jokes from an Off Broadway show I saw last week called *Old Jews Telling Jokes*?"

"No," she said.

"Why not?" I pleaded.

"Because you aren't a Jew," she noted.

Audits

Mandy had a policy that anyone interested in her classes could audit one session for thirty-five dollars. This resulted in a series of one-time visitors to class who often provided an element of humor and/or pathos. One young handsome Hispanic male attended, and Mandy immediately asked him, "Why do you want to be here?"

"I want to see what it is all about," he stammered.

"That isn't an answer," she said.

"Well, someone recommended this class," he continued.

"But what is your goal here?" Mandy pursued.

No response. He took part in the floor exercise with leg flop that day. Mandy was unmerciful on him, and after thirty minutes, yes thirty minutes, of trying and retrying, she ordered him, "Go sit down.

Another man who had a Russian accent attended one day, and Mandy asked him to visualize a room and the emotions it evoked. "I'm ready," he said after a few minutes. "I see the pipes above the stage; the pictures on the walls; the dark, dirty floor …"

"Stop!" Mandy screeched. "I didn't mean this room."

He was done for the day.

Another day, a young man showed up wearing the most perfect denim outfit that I had ever seen. Perfectly pressed denim pants had large, carefully rolled-up cuffs. A denim shirt and nifty denim jacket completed the ensemble. His hair was jet black, neatly parted, and slicked into place with what might have been Wildroot Cream Oil. "Why don't you sit down over there by the window," Mandy guided.

In the daylight from the window, he appeared to be from that wonderful 1950s era. After eying him for some time, Mandy told him, "You will have no trouble getting work, even if you are a terrible actor." She continued, "You have an intriguing appearance and can be on the set with no speaking part simply to add atmosphere. In the business they call people like you furniture."

He never returned. In fact, none of the above auditors returned.

What Was Really Going on Here?

For the most part, I am a thoughtful person; however, not always. In retrospect, it is clear that I did not grasp the deeper issues at play during my fall with Mandy. In fact, it is helpful for me to write this story so that I can learn some lessons, even at age seventy-one.

I would not call this experience a clash of the titans. Neither of us approached titan status, although we probably thought we did. I also would not declare a winner of a galactic struggle for power and righteousness. Rather it was a situation in which two bright, stubborn, successful, and very different types of people spent a fall together in an intense setting. In looking back, I see that my naïve approach to taking acting lessons made this a highly inefficient experience, amplifying my frustration. At the time, I felt that I was a natural and needn't bother with much preparation. In fact, I believed that Mandy might have felt uncomfortable with how good I was. I came to believe that I just needed to get into the hands of an excellent and supportive teacher, and I would become a hit.

Had I taken the time and effort to do some homework, prepare for class, and try to understand the history and theory of method acting, much of this may have had a different outcome. Instead, I developed a me-versus-them attitude, the result of which was to fight the system, question the teaching, and make no additional effort to improve my understanding. Mandy and I shared the 'if I said it, it must be right' attitude. Mandy and I had this in common, but little else. She is a visionary, a romantic, a mystic like William Blake … "Tiger, tiger burning bright, in the forests of the night." I am a scientist, an academic, an empiricist like John Locke … "No man's knowledge here can go beyond his experience." Just as Mandy made me uncomfortable, I am sure that I made her uncomfortable. She never would look at me during her chats. She asked who I voted for and then answered the question herself. She continued to ask me every week, "Are you just along for the ride?"

And I would always respond, "No, I want to work in the business."

"How much outside reading and preparation are you doing?" she asked one day.

"Not much," I confessed.

She assigned me a book, and I read it. However, the next week she brought in four additional books that she wanted the class to consider buying. I bought none. On and on it went until the final straw.

After completing the last class of my package, on a cold December night just before Christmas, Mandy asked me, "Are you planning to sign up for another package of classes?"

"Things are getting busier at work (I had just been rehired)," I told her, "and it is going to be hard to make the Tuesday afternoon classes."

She said she hoped I could return but advised me that she had just instituted a new tuition policy. She was going to charge for her classes in a tiered fashion, such that those who were better off financially would pay a higher fee. I decided not to inquire how she would adjudicate the new policy.

The Writing Workshop

"Say What You Mean Before You Die"

"Why don't you look into the Marsh Theater programs?" my writing tutor asked me.

As my interest in the arts, both written and performing, has grown, I have sought advice on next steps. I knew vaguely about the Marsh, but no details at all. The next day was Saturday, and I went to Marsh on the web. Perhaps by karma, a writing workshop was being offered the very next day from 10:00 a.m. to 4:00 p.m. The course was to be taught by Charlie Varon, whose bio said he had been writing "for page and stage" for over forty years. Committing the better part of my Sunday to writing felt right, and I registered for the course, which was titled, "Say What You Mean Before You Die."

The Marsh Theater building is located at 1062 Valencia Street in the Mission District of San Francisco. The Mission District is a colorful neighborhood, inhabited primarily by Spanish speaking peoples from various countries. While some avoid the Mission for various reasons, I find it to be one of the most genuine and interesting neighborhoods in San Francisco.

As I climbed out of my UberX car, I noticed a worn and shabby appearance to the buildings on the street. Some had posters, torn and dirty, hanging from the front doors. The posters were announcing events long-since finished. The Marsh Theater had two separate entrances, one of which looked open for business. I walked in, and despite it being 10:00 a.m., I was immediately enveloped in darkness. I also noted a distinctive coldness in the room. As my eyes were adjusting, I was warmly greeted by a woman. "Hi, I am Rebecca. I will be helping Charlie today," she said. "Just sign in on this sheet, go on into the studio, and sit wherever you like."

By now, I could see that the studio consisted of three tiered rows of seats upholstered with red fabric. Among about forty seats, my classmates occupied about ten. I sat down near a foursome of men who were engaged in discussion. "I just stand up and talk, and if something funny comes out, that is a good thing," a slender, balding, and bespectacled man said.

"Well, I do data management as my day job but play music and tell stories at clubs in the evenings," said another middle-age man.

The discussion went on as if I wasn't there. Each man seemed to be experienced in some form of performance. I wondered why they were attending a writing workshop. I began to develop a bit of uneasiness. Was I in the right place? I also noted that my wardrobe did not fit well with my classmates.

I have taken courses in the Mission in the past, so much of this was not new to me. The lack of heat was unpleasant but typical of these studio rooms. Also, the black-painted walls and dim lighting was to be expected. I also knew that I did not own a wardrobe that would meet the dress code for such gatherings. As I looked around at my classmates, I noted the usual odd hairdos, the ubiquitous blue jeans, and the odd shirts and hats being worn indoors. Backpacks were everywhere. In contrast, I do not own a pair of blue jeans, nor do I own a backpack. My shirts are oxfords from Nordstrom and my hair, what is left, is neatly trimmed. I guess this is one reason that I am usually ignored in such gatherings.

Charlie Varon joined us promptly at 10:00 a.m. and settled into a hard-back chair in front of the seating area. A spotlight flooded the area of his chair with bright stage light and allowed me to see every nuance of body language. Here was a guy comfortable in his skin and eager to offer us what he could. He was dressed in blue jeans and a red pullover sweater. He had a short dark beard and an ever-so-receding hairline. His body language was positive, and he instilled confidence in me that I might learn something. Rebecca joined him, sitting silently in a chair to his left. Other than plugging her writing club in Berkeley, she remained silent.

"Welcome to the workshop everyone. I've been doing this same program for about twenty years, and it is usually enjoyable for all involved. By the way, let me apologize for how cold it is in the studio. We just turned on the heat, and it should warm up in two or three hours," Charlie told us.

People had settled down and were paying close attention.

"You may be curious about the name of the workshop," Charlie continued. "This is actually a quote that my partner and mentor, David Ford, came up with during a radio interview. Asked what our goals were at Marsh, David said we teach acting and writing. When pushed about the writing lessons, he said, 'We encourage people to say what they mean before they die,'" Charlie explained.

Suddenly a woman sitting in the front row raised her hand and blurted out, "Could I make a comment about your introduction?"

This person was a small, middle-aged woman dressed in army-style camouflage pants, a sweatshirt, and what appeared to be a hand-knit wool ski cap. "Ehhhh … no," Charlie replied. "I want to keep the flow of ideas going for now."

The camouflaged woman squirmed in her seat and appeared reluctant to keep her thoughts to herself, but she managed to do so.

"Let's dig right in and do some writing," Charlie continued. "First, I want everyone to get out of your seats and join me in this open stage area. I want you to walk around and imagine a song in your mind. This can be any song and any message. Then I want you to write about whatever thoughts and feelings you take from the song."

I had never heard the term *prompt*, but that is what we had received. We were given a prompt for writing our first piece of the day.

A vigorous rush to the stage area ensued. It was clear that these people needn't be asked twice to prance around stage. As I walked normally, I noted the unusual walking styles employed by others. There was skipping, head bobbing, eyes popping, and even sideways and backward pacing. Suddenly, as might occur in a game of musical chairs, Charlie said, "Okay, stop and go to your seats and write."

My choice of song was "Stand by Me." This is the theme song from the 1986 movie of the same name directed by Rob Reiner. The movie is an American drama based on the Stephen King novella, "The Body," which tells a poignant story of a young boy, Gordie, just on the verge of adolescence, who along with three friends, discovers the body of a dead boy while walking in the woods. He has never seen a dead person and probably has given little though to death in his young years. Eyes wide with a combination of fear and excitement, Gordie and his friends run back to their little town. Now they are all in it together, although they really don't quite know what to do. They all agree that they must stand by one another. This is a profound awakening for Gordie and haunts him throughout his life.

Based on this, I wrote an essay called "Stand by Me:"

If you stand by me, I will show you death. At first, I was afraid. Later it was new and important. Then I needed it.

I am older now. I remember boys, but girls could be okay. Come with me all you men ... Ok, now I know death is everywhere ... my tribe is with me and stands by me.

Look, I see it again, and it is almost cold.

Look, a young boy. Come stand by me.

I am one now. How odd.

I didn't think that this short piece was too subtle, with the young boy's lifelong obsession ending with him becoming the dead body. However, as will be seen, I was wrong.

Charlie prompted us again, saying, "I want you to write about something that bugs you."

I decided to write an essay called "Service."

Service is a relative term. Not only is service relative, it is highly subjective. Sometimes I take bad service personally. I can be insecure about service. Am I too preppy? Am I too shy? Am I too short? Am I too impatient? Am I just paranoid?

Alcohol and service are soul mates. The time lapse between sitting down at a restaurant and a glass of wine or cocktail showing up on the table is something I track with a stopwatch. For me, all service improves upon the successful and expected delivery of my drink.

At this point, Charlie broke into our writing and added another prompt on top of the original prompt, "I want you to introduce a new person into your essay who has even a stronger opinion about whatever it is that bugs you."

Compared to me, Tony is far more serious about service in restaurants. Tony can become a monster. His base behavior is being bossy and differential to waiters. One minor slip up and things become so unpleasant that everyone at the table begins to squirm.

Tony is good for me. I realize how to put service into perspective. I can take a deep breath. I can look the other way. I can leave a bigger tip—anyway. Service is a point in time, and only that; just one point in a long life.

When we had completed two essays, Charlie instructed, "Please find a partner and read one of your two essays to him or her for comments. Then switch."

I have always disliked pairing up with unknown partners or breakout groups to share ideas. I am inherently shy, and I also don't trust unknown partners to add much value. This occasion was no exception.

I was startled by how quickly my classmates paired up. In short order, I found that there was only one person left to serve as my partner. That turned out to be the woman in the camouflaged pants and ski cap. "Would you be my partner?" I hesitantly asked her after moving next to her chair.

She seemed reluctant, but short of boycotting the exercise, she had no choice. Also, I wondered whether she felt uneasy about having interrupted Charlie's introduction.

"Would you like to share your piece first?" I invited in my most polite tone.

"I didn't know we were going to be asked to do this. I can't read my piece to you," she stuttered.

At this point she was almost trembling. Her eyes were wide and defensive. "Why not?" I asked.

"Well, I wrote about sexual stuff, and I was the man," she mumbled. "You can go ahead and read both of yours to me."

By now, there was only time for me to read one, so I read "Stand by Me." "Did you understand that?" I inquired.

"No," she replied.

Suddenly, Charlie's voice rang out, "Okay, I would like each of you to come up front individually and read a ninety-second excerpt from your favorite of the two pieces you have prepared. It isn't required, but is encouraged."

I decided to read from my service essay rather than from what now appeared to be the inscrutable "Stand by Me."

Judging from the reaction of my classmates, they did find some mild humor in my work. In turn, their performances were more creative and suggested past training. For example, some presenters appeared to have a style. Loud, accented speech or slurred, barely intelligible speech were used. Some gestured wildly and pranced around the stage as they presented. I noticed that a number of my classmates spoke to Charlie by name and that he addressed them by name. I realized that I was swimming with an experienced group.

The workshop progressed with more prompts, resulting in three more essays. "Picture yourself at your own funeral eavesdropping on a conversation between friends about you," Charlie prompted. "Then another person enters the conversation and sets them straight on what you are really like."

His subsequent prompts were, "Think about a time that a younger person asked you for some important advice. After you write about this, find the most important phrase from that essay and write another essay focusing on the important implications of that phrase."

In all, we produced five essays, and while exhausted, I was pleased at how the writing flowed for me.

As with any conference, one of the highlights was lunch. At 1:00 p.m., Charlie said, "Go ahead and take forty-five minutes for lunch, but be back at one forty-five sharp."

Having spent little time in this neighborhood, I was unsure of where to go. I was tired and hungry after all the writing, so I decided I needed something substantial. I wandered down one street and then another. Numerous places were closed on Sunday with strong but rusty-looking bars securing their windows. Finally, I came across a 'ole-in-the wall place with pictures of sandwiches on the window. It was difficult to tell whether the place was open or not. I tried the door and entered to find a long, narrow room with a single Formica-topped lunch counter extending the length of the room. Behind the counter were a small Chinese woman and a large Chinese man. She appeared to be the server and he the cook. There were only two customers at the counter, both male and both speaking animated Spanish as they nursed their coffee. I ordered a cheeseburger with fries, which was priced at a reasonable nine dollars. The Chinese man went to work at his grill, and soon the woman delivered my lunch. It was surprisingly good. Mission accomplished, and with renewed energy, I returned by 1:45 p.m. sharp.

We did some more writing after lunch and then we spent the last hour talking strategy. The messages from Charlie took the form of a pep talk. We need to write consistently. We need not be overly discouraged by criticism of our work, which could in some cases be rude. And we should beware of writers' block. He finished by handing out a card with writing tips, such as: always try to exceed your abilities; don't be reluctant to ask for help; and be confident in your work.

By now, I knew that I was the rookie in the group. I listened as the questions from my classmates dealt with more technical aspects of writing and publishing than I had considered. This only made me more excited to make progress. As I left for the day, Charlie came over, shook my hand, and said, "It was great having you today, Jim. I hope you find this helpful for your work."

I was now on a first-name basis. I had graduated.

The Wake-Up Call

The sore throat started, as usual, in the middle of the night. I have always marveled at how infrequently I need to swallow when I am in bed for the night. In fact, while I don't know for sure, I doubt if I swallow at all when I am asleep. Once a sore throat takes hold, however, it seems for some reason that I need to swallow at least once a minute. I begin to worry ahead of each new swallow. I begin to count the swallows. Worst of all, each swallow becomes more uncomfortable than the next until the swallows are actually painful. This time, I ended up hardly able to swallow all of my saliva in one swallow due to what felt like a swollen uvula. The uvula is that tab of flesh that dangles down in the back of your mouth and seems to serve no purpose at all. When swollen, the uvula actually becomes a concern for adequate breathing and swallowing. I began to wonder how big my uvula had become. I was torn between trying to sleep and curiosity driving me to jump out of bed, find a flashlight, and examine the size of my uvula. I decided that trying to sleep would put my body in a better position to fight off the impending cold.

Upon waking after a fitful night with my sore throat and swollen uvula, I wondered if it would be a go for the planned ski trip departure today. My wife and I were planning on flying up to my home state of Oregon and spending three days at a wonderful resort called Sun River. During this time, we would ski two days at a nearby ski area called Mount Bachelor ski area. This trip was particularly meaningful to me as we were returning to an area where I first learned to ski some sixty years ago and where we used to take our children to ski during their spring breaks. I did not want to cancel the trip because of my sore throat.

"Well, this is the big day," I said to my wife as cheerfully as I could muster.

"Yes, but you look a bit pale," she replied.

"Oh, I feel okay; let's finish packing and head for the airport," I responded with as much enthusiasm as is possible when it hurts to talk.

I knew that if I told my wife what was really going on, that would be the end of the trip. Even with my age of seventy-three, I felt that I was in robust health and no way could a simple sore throat derail this long-awaited trip.

As the plane descended into the Bend-Redmond Airport, I was struck by the sheer majesty of the snow-capped Cascade mountain range. I did my best to ignore my sore throat, anticipating the wonderful time coming up instead.

"Why does your voice sound funny?" my wife asked, pulling me out of my daydreams.

"I didn't know it did," I replied in the best voice I could muster up.

We picked up our rental car and drove twenty minutes into the charming town of Bend, Oregon.

During the drive, I tried hard to swallow as normally as possible. I was keenly aware that my wife was now watching my every move. She suspected that something was up.

"Well, I have a confession to make," I blurted out as we ate hamburgers at the venerable Pine Tavern, circa 1935.

"What?" she mumbled through a bite.

"I have a sore throat," I said, trying to be nonchalant.

Her reaction was a combination of concern and irritation. "Why didn't you tell me, and then we could have postponed the trip? You aren't a spring chicken anymore, either," she threw in, playing the age card.

"Do you know where the nearest drugstore is?" I inquired of the hostess at the Pine Tavern as we departed.

"There is a Walgreens only a few minutes from here," she directed.

I found the Cepacol throat lozenges and stocked up for the day. After a few minutes of sucking on the first lozenge, I felt better and convinced myself that coming on this trip was a good idea.

By dinnertime, my nose was running. This is, for me, the natural progression of a cold, and I was ready for the next move. "Let's go back to Walgreens after dinner," I requested of my wife.

I knew that this request would increase her scrutiny and decrease my chance of skiing, or at least skiing without constant vigil.

Walgreens visit number two for the day produced a box of Sudafed decongestants. I was loading up for a two-day battle. After wolfing down a double dose of Sudafed, I slept pretty well through the night.

As I woke up the next morning, I noted my wife peering at me. "How do you feel?" was her first utterance.

"I have no idea, I need to get up and move around," I responded, uncertain myself about how I felt.

"Well, there will be no skiing if you are worse," she predictably stated.

No skiing! I was heading to holy ground. I was heading to my historic skiing roots. Please, I said to my body, let me be okay. Even after getting up, I wasn't really sure how I felt. The sore throat was better, but the runny nose was worse and I felt a bit dizzy. Needless to say, I did not provide this level of detail to my wife. I downed some more Sudafed, and we headed over to the lodge for breakfast. I had a healthy breakfast of orange juice and oatmeal. It would be a go for skiing this morning.

"Shouldn't we just check out our rentals for one day and buy a one-day lift ticket?" my wife suggested.

"It's cheaper if we get a two-day rental and ticket, and I'm sure that I can make it for both days," I assured her.

I had no idea whether I could really make it through two days, but I wanted to plan for success. From this moment on, the rest of the day seemed to move in slow motion. We finally got our first run down the slope at 11:00 a.m. That is the latest first ski run I have had in my life. And then it began. At first, I ignored the burning and weakness in the front part of my thighs, ascribing it to needing some warm-up runs. After all, I was seventy-three years old, had a cold, and hadn't skied in over a year. But was this the beginning of a wake-up call? After two more runs, it was clear that this weakness was not going away with a few warm-up runs. Now I was worried.

We skied back to the lodge and bought our lunch. I became immersed in thoughts, some verging on paranoia. Damn this cheapskate ski area for not grooming the slopes more carefully. It must be the thick, loose snow that was causing me trouble. But why was everyone else gliding along without complaint? I guess I am to blame. I failed to condition my legs properly for the trip. Also, I am weak from the cold. My nose is running, and a slight cough is setting in. But, of course, my real fear was that I was getting too old to ski. Age had caught up with my thighs. Was this my ski version of a wake-up call? How can I determine which of these explanations was truth? Will I ever ski again?

Heading out for the afternoon runs, I was hoping that my thighs would suddenly come alive and that the morning was all a bad dream. But, sure enough, the burning and weakness persisted. Now the bright sun, the pain, the exhaustion, the loose snow, and the fears all blended into a blur, and I began to hallucinate. I dropped a glove, but decided that I couldn't, or even didn't want, to pick it up. My wife came over, picked it up, and handed it to me. "What in the heck is wrong with you?" she said with a tone of annoyance and anxiety in her voice.

The next thing I remember is coming back to our hotel room. The cough had clearly established itself as the next stage of my cold. I began attacking the cough with Halls cough drops. I was not a good companion the rest of the day and evening. I was immersed in thought and anxious for the next day. I had much to find out.

On our final day of skiing, the first run was at 11:15 a.m., a new record for late start. Unfortunately, either my age or my cold again led to weak legs. I took only a few runs before suggesting a lunch break. As I settled into my place at the table, I uttered in audible tones, "I cannot believe that my body has deteriorated this much in one year."

"I feel the same way," chirped a woman sitting just behind me at the next table.

I turned to see a fiftyish red-haired lady with a big smile on her face. "Yah, but I am seventy-three years old," I retorted.

"Then you're kickin' it," she said in a reassuring tone.

I did not feel better. We headed out for the afternoon, and I wondered how I would make it through the day.

As it turned out, I soon began to feel dizzy, weak, and light-headed. Nevertheless, I skied on. I saw some strange things that afternoon. Just ahead of me in the lift line was a large, overweight young man wearing a purple tutu. With him was the Cat in the Hat from Dr. Seuss's book of the same name. I never realized how tall and how ugly the Cat in the Hat was until that moment. I don't know whether I was hallucinating, but I hope so.

For some reason, on my last run of the afternoon, I imagined that my legs felt a little better.

We arose early the next morning to head to the airport. "How do you feel today?" my wife asked immediately.

"Well, the best I can say is that I don't feel worse," I replied, halfway believing it.

As our Bombardier Q400 plane began its descent into Oakland Airport, I knew that I could not yet answer the fundamental question. Was this remarkable decline in my leg strength due to aging, or was it simply being weak from a bad cold? I vowed to find the answer. As we approached the airport by flying over the bay and some beautiful green rolling hills, I congratulated myself. I had skied two days. I knew that I would return next year and prove to myself that without a bad cold, I was as good as ever.

After landing, I paid a quick visit to the men's room. While washing my hands, I glanced into the mirror. I still looked the same.

Things Are Not What They Seem

Rio Olympic Games, 2016

At age seventy-three, I certainly do not consider myself old. However, after spending a week at the Olympic Games in Rio de Janeiro, it is clear that everyone else does.

Being offered seats on the bus and subway was my first eye opener. In the United States, the occasional polite person will offer his or her seat to a handicapped or even older individual. That is the exception, not the rule. Most of the time, the typical seated passenger on a subway will pretend to be asleep or reading intently when a candidate for his or her seat approaches. In Rio, it was just the opposite. People literally were jumping out of their seats to give them to my wife and me, apparently because we were old. And as far as the blue-colored seats marked for special people on subways, almost never was there someone breaching the local contract with the elderly and infirmed.

"You deprived that young girl of great pleasure," said the stern middle-age woman.

"What are you talking about?" I responded.

Then it was clear. A few minutes earlier, a young girl had smiled at me as I stood in the train aisle and waved at me to take her seat. I waved her off, thanking her, but secretly being somewhat offended that she thought I was too old to stand. When she finally got up and left the train, I did sit down in her seat. This is when the stern lady sitting to my right began her lecture.

"Here in Brazil, children are taught at an early age that it is not just polite but a privilege to give their seats to the elderly," the stern woman continued. "That young lady would have remembered her act of generosity fondly for the rest of the day."

I was speechless, but I had been taught a lesson that stayed with me the remainder of the trip. A) I am old, and B) the elderly can expect a win-win proposition on buses and subway trains. Not only can they sit, they can make others happy.

As the days went by, my wife and I became aggressive toward getting seats. We even began standing directly in front of seated younger people and staring at them until they saw us and responded. We became entitled passengers. Woe to any unqualified person we would find sitting in the special blue seats. The problem of long rides on public transportation had been solved. Unfortunately, nothing could be done about our aging.

Attending events meant lining up for security checks and having your ticket examined. For some reason, my wife and I were frequently directed into a special line called Priority. These were much shorter lines, and the implication was that for some reason we were deemed important people. We did wear our tickets in plastic lanyards draped around our necks. Perhaps this looked official and important. Perhaps we were media types.

"Boy, aren't those priority lines handy?" an elderly American asked us while riding on the subway.

"Yes, but I don't know why we are being flagged as important people," I answered.

"That's simple: you are old," he said. "The Olympic organizers set those lines up specifically for those fans appearing to be over sixty-five years of age."

After the rigor of the first day attending events, I became more accepting of my advanced years. The temperature was ninety degrees, as was the humidity. Upon arrival at Olympic Park, after a ninety-minute trip on the newly built Line 4 subway, followed by a special bus, we walked up a flight of about fifty stairs. At the top of the stairs, a sign directed us to Olympic Park. Another sign, labeled RioCentro, pointed us in the opposite direction. We agreed, our destination was Olympic Park, and we headed that way.

Olympic Park was much larger than I had imagined, with numerous buildings spreading out in all directions. Some of the buildings, including the aquatic center, were built for the Pan-American Games of 2007. The notion, often implied in press stories, that Rio started from scratch to build the entire infrastructure for the Olympic Games was certainly not true. We walked about one mile just to reach the security entrance gates.

"You are in the wrong place," said the attendant upon examining our tickets. "You are supposed to be at RioCentro, not here."

"Where is RioCentro?" I gasped, exhausted, dripping sweat, and vaguely recalling the confusing signage we had seen on the stairs.

"Oh, that is about a three-mile walk back that way," she gestured in the direction from whence we came.

We had misunderstood the signage on the stairway, which was easy to do. About forty minutes later, we struggled up the final path to RioCentro. We arrived in our seats hot, dehydrated, and about an hour after the event had started. I apologized to my wife for the mistake in organizing our day. She didn't blame me at all. She did tell me later that the table tennis (ping pong) match we attended at RioCentro was her least favorite event among the nine different events that we attended.

The tickets for our evening event of track and field listed the starting time as 5:45 p.m. The venue would be Olympic Stadium, which was located in a completely different part of the city. Like much of Olympic Park, Olympic Stadium was not built for these games, rather was the site of track and field events for the Pan-American Games. I mention this again, as there was a not-so-subtle campaign in the press to criticize as much of the Rio and Olympic organizing committees' decisions as possible. Wasting money on building infrastructure in a third-world country was just one of the many themes.

Being our first trip to Olympic Stadium, I was uncertain how much time to budget for the trip. Given the events of the day, such as arriving an hour late for our first event of the games, I decided to be conservative and leave plenty of time for travel.

"Let's leave on the early side, just to be safe," I suggested to my wife.

"Okay, how early?" she asked.

"Well, if the event starts at five forty-five; why don't we leave at four thirty?" I said.

We arrived at Olympic Stadium about 5:30 p.m.

This trip had involved a subway ride followed by a train ride. Again, all was smooth, but the distances were long. Fortunately, some younger passengers gave up their seats for us.

As we approached the entrance, we heard drums and music. Things seemed quite festive around the stadium. Security was also in evidence with numerous trucks and armed soldiers standing around. We concentrated on the musicians and gaily dressed dancers rather than the soldiers.

We found our way to our seats. It was now exactly 5:45 p.m. … mission accomplished. However, as we looked around, we were puzzled to see only a few hundred people in a stadium with a 60,000-person seating capacity. I carefully scanned our printed program and slowly understood that I had once again misunderstood what to do. Listed at 5:45 p.m. was a medal ceremony followed by some low-key, preliminary high jumps for the decathlon event. Medal ceremonies last about five minutes and simply involve the gold, silver, and bronze medal winners from a prior event to mount a podium, receive their medals, and wait as a recording of the national anthem of the gold medal winner is played over the PA system. Another medal ceremony was planned for some time later. Bottom line … no important events were scheduled until about 8:30 p.m. We were basically almost three hours too early.

For the second time that day, I apologized to my wife for a mistake in planning. Again, she said not to worry about it. "Well, how about a beer?" I asked.

We left our seats, went out to the grounds around the stadium, drank a beer, and killed about three hours. As it turned out, the wait was well worth it.

Did we see Babe Ruth? Did we see Joe Montana? Did we see Michael Jordan? No, but we did see arguably the most charismatic athlete in the world that night. The Jamaican superstar sprinter, Usain Bolt, was running in the finals of the men's 200-meter dash. Usain is a man among boys, standing six feet five inches, a full head taller than his rivals in the race. He winked, danced, and pointed here and there before lining up. Then he touched his finger to his lips to silence his crowd. He pranced to the win in the 200-meter dash, collecting another gold medal. This was his third Olympic Games over the past eight years, and he was on the way to winning a total of three gold medals … again … underscoring just how special this evening was. Those three hours of idle people-watching were a distant memory.

By now, we were beginning to relax. We had been in Rio for two full days and, despite the scare stories propagated by the press, had not yet seen a single mosquito. Nor had we been mugged. The press had been unmerciful ahead of the Olympics, attempting to plant fear of numerous things in visitors' minds. It is hard to estimate how many potential Olympic lovers stayed away due to these bogus articles. As for the athletes, several of the top male golfers in the world begged off the Olympics voicing fear of zika virus infection. It is hard to contract the mosquito-borne zika infection without mosquitoes, however. By the end of our week in Rio, we still had not seen a mosquito, had not been mugged, had not seen a half-finished and unusable venue, had not had a walkway collapse on us, and had not heard of a single sailor on the bay contracting a gastrointestinal disease. In fact, upon winning the gold medal in sailing, the Brazilian team jumped into the water of the bay and swam around to celebrate.

My wife and I are pretty interested in fine dining, and we usually explore the top restaurants wherever we go. I had spent hours researching the top choices in our hotel neighborhood, near Ipanema beach. As it turned out, however, due to the late start of the evening events and the long train ride back, we generally didn't arrive in our hotel neighborhood ready for dinner until around midnight. By then, a quick simple dinner and bed were the only thing to do. All my research was for naught.

As we sat on the outdoor balcony of a restaurant on our last night, we finally saw *The Man from Ipanema*. Everyone has heard the iconic song written by Stan Getz in 1962 called "The Girl from Ipanema."

Tall and tan and young and lovely

The girl from Ipanema goes walking and

When she passes, each one she passes goes "ah"

Well, we did not pass the girl, but we did meet a character from our Ipanema neighborhood who certainly was unique in his own right. I first noticed him across the street wandering back and forth in front of a different restaurant. He was scantily dressed in old shorts, sandals, and no shirt. While I couldn't make out the tune, he was carrying a large metal drum and appeared to be beating out a rhythm. I turned away, happy that he was on the other side of the street. Time passed, our courses arrived, and we took our first bites. Suddenly, the sound of the old man's voice and his rendition of "The Girl from Ipanema," accompanied by drum, were on the sidewalk right next to us. He had crossed the street to serenade us. I have heard this song many times over the years but never done the way he did it. It was thin voiced and did not carefully follow the melody. The words were spot on however, and it seemed to be the only song he knew or at least wanted to play.

"This is really annoying, isn't it?" I asked my wife.

"Is it, really?" she responded thoughtfully.

What was her point? And then I knew.

The Rio we had experienced was a land of music, poverty, beauty, and friendly people. The poor man playing music for us smiled and held out his hat.

Lessons from an Airplane

Flying a private plane never even crossed my mind until a friend told me he was learning to fly. He raved about the experience, although he did admit it was taking a fair amount of his time. When he related this, I was sixty-four years old, and he was not much younger. Had he been young, I would have discounted the activity as a young man's sport. However, given our similar ages, I paid attention. Now, from this vantage point, I can also see that this notion of learning to fly played into my growing need to find some new hobbies and activities to fill time as I slowed down my working pace. If my friend could do it, perhaps so could I.

"It will be like drinking from a fire hose," instructor Dave explained during my informational interview at Palo Alto Airport. Having been a good student my entire life, this did not dissuade me at all.

What were the costs? Beyond the financial commitment was a far bigger personal commitment. I would need to demonstrate a level of discipline not required since my earlier days of medical school training and later generating my salary by acquiring federal research grants. Regular flying lessons were mandatory. These involved showing up at the airport on time two to three times a week and working for two to three hours with both ground and flying instruction. I did this while working a full-time job. My routine was to load the coffee maker the night before and set the alarm for 5:45 a.m. In the morning, I would hop out of bed, start the coffee maker, get dressed, and by 6:00 a.m. head out the door with my coffee and breakfast to eat in the car. The breakfast was always the same, a warmed-up frozen waffle topped with butter and jam and wrapped in a paper towel to keep warm. Frankly, this all tasted pretty good as I drove the fifty minutes to the Palo Alto Airport.

Arriving at around 6:50 a.m., I would run out to the tarmac and preflight the plane: untying the security ropes, checking the gas and oil levels, and in the winter, deicing the wing surfaces using towels wetted down with hot water. The plane was a standard single-engine Cessna 172 with a 180 horsepower engine, two seats in front, and two seats in back. Top speed was about 120 knots, and typical flying altitude was between 3,000 and 6,000 feet. At precisely 7:00 a.m., my instructor would drive into the parking lot and we would go to work.

Try doing this two to three times a week for one year at age sixty-four. On top of this, I had homework, which involved another two to three hours of home study a week. Remember, the FAA flight test for becoming a private pilot involves both flying knowledge and skill, but it also requires passing a rigorous written exam. There is no easy path to a private pilot's license. I needed to maintain a laser focus on my training. Sure, I occasionally felt discouraged. But a supportive instructor helped me push on. And once licensed, I needed to maintain my skills through frequent flying. I flew virtually every weekend for six years. My wife accompanied me on most flights. When I retired, I had logged 560 hours in the air and performed over 1,200 landings.

Maneuvers

It might be surprising to you—it was certainly surprising to me—that in addition to the obvious flying skills of takeoffs and landings, there turned out to be a series of exercises known as maneuvers. These maneuvers are necessary in special circumstances that might arise unexpectedly and pose a safety hazard. It was essential that I master these skills.

Steep Turns

As a new pilot, I had to learn to perform steep turns just in case I was ever trapped in a crowded air space approaching a busy airport. While originally this hadn't occurred to me as an essential skill, I came to recognize that learning this maneuver made sense. By performing steep turns, I could maintain my position while occupying minimal air space.

The definition of steep is to bank your airplane to 45 degrees for the turn. A steep turn involves bringing the airspeed of the airplane down to a cruise speed somewhat slower than usual. You then line up on a distant target, perhaps a mountaintop or a radio tower. You set your bug, a movable marker on your compass, to line up with the target. Then you note your exact altitude.

To complete the exercise, you bank the plane either right or left, and complete a 360-degree turn. As you level off, you need to be back at the spot of origin, within one hundred feet of your original altitude, and headed no more than 10 degrees off your original target, as marked by the bug.

It seemed to me that the method to complete the turn and remain at the same altitude throughout would be to keep my eye on the altimeter. Based upon observing the altimeter, I could make frequent adjustments to the up or down pitch of the plane during the turn, hopefully keeping the plane at the correct altitude. While this seemed the logical technique, that was not the case. In fact, practicing this maneuver, I learned that some things are not what they seem. Until I realized this, I continued to fail, overshooting above and below the desired altitude throughout the maneuver—and almost never arriving within one hundred feet of my original altitude.

If what you think is the obvious solution to a problem keeps failing, you better rethink what you are doing. In the case of steep turns, I had to learn never to look down at the altimeter on the panel, as I would expect to do, but rather to fix my eyes on the distant horizon as I progressed around the 360 degrees. I simply had to keep the horizon fixed in my visual field at the same level throughout the turn and, voila, I arrived back at the original altitude.

In my own life, things are certainly not always what they seem. A few years ago, I thought my boss was well-regarded in the organization. After all, he was the CEO, and I wanted to make sure that I was closely associated with him. I accepted his invitations to join him and other close associates for weekday lunches and even dinners. I thought that by doing this, I would be well-placed for promotion. Little if any business was transacted during these meals however, a clue that things might not be as they seemed. I became more cautious, begging off on these outings with him. Then one day, my office door flew open and the general counsel for the company entered. "I wanted to let you know that we are letting your boss go, along with several of his closest associates."

Slow Flight

"What is your least favorite part of flying instruction?" I asked my instructor one day.

"Slow flight," he replied.

"Tell me why," I asked.

"Because it is boring," he mumbled.

That reply certainly influenced my way of thinking about this maneuver. In fact, I began to take slow flight lightly.

But I found that slow flight is anything but boring. In fact, it ended up being my most challenging maneuver. Slow flight gives the pilot a way to slow the plane down to the slowest possible speed yet maintain flight. This comes in handy when you are following another plane in the airport traffic pattern, which usually consists of a parade of three or four planes circling around the airport, one behind the other, waiting for their turn to land. If the plane ahead of you is flying slower than expected, employing slow flight can help maintain adequate spacing between this plane and your own.

You perform slow flight by bringing your airspeed down to about 40 knots. At this speed, by dropping down full flaps, you maintain adequate lift. Keep in mind that normal cruising speed is about 120 knots in the plane that I flew. The FAA standard for the maneuver is to hold your direction of flight within 10 degrees and to maintain a constant altitude within one hundred feet. Doing this, the nose of the plane ends up being pointed high and the plane is quite unsteady, since it is being asked to perform at the very edge of its performance characteristics. Once I realized that I was neglecting practicing slow flight—and performing it poorly whenever I tried it—I reversed course and practiced over and over until I became really good at it. Knowing what I now do, I would call this maneuver tense and hard rather than boring.

I can recall similar instances in my life where a biased comment or underestimation led to my poor performance. In grade school, older students told me that addition was easy. Then during class competition doing serial addition at the blackboard, I finished last in the class. Embarrassed and determined to improve—I learned then just how competitive I was—I had my mother drill me at home. She would fire serial numbers at me, I would write them down and then add them as we went along. I mastered this skill to become best in class.

No one hands you these successes. You have to fight for them. Later in life, when I was a medical student, an upperclassman told me that reading electrocardiograms was easy and boring. Again, I approached this important and challenging task with a poor attitude. The results were predictable: I took twice as long learning this process as expected. Eventually I found myself having to ask for assistance during night call. It became clear to me that a skillful reading can distinguish between a true heart attack and something more benign. This turned out to be a lifesaving skill, and eventually I became quite good at it. And it was anything but easy and boring.

Stalls

The power-off stall maneuver is quite anxiety-producing for some, but I took to it well. In simple terms, a stall is when the plane no longer has enough lift to keep it flying. The result is a steep drop of the nose, and if nothing is done, the plane spirals to the ground. Losing lift is usually due to an imbalance between speed and wing angle. Slower speed and higher-pitched wings are bad news.

The stall maneuver is meant to mimic what might happen if I approached the runway for landing and noticed that I might not make it to the runway. By pulling back on the yolk and lifting the nose of the plane, I might hope to extend my flying distance and reach the runway. While this seems intuitive, it would be exactly the wrong thing to do. The more the nose is pulled up, the slower the plane speed, and the greater the pitch of the wings. This vicious cycle usually results in a sudden stall, and if I were near the ground, I would impact terrain, flying lingo for a crash landing.

I learned that the proper thing to do if I felt that I might not make it to the runway is to increase power. At a slow speed, such as on a landing approach, I would gain added altitude and flight distance by adding power, not by raising the nose of the plane. Or, if I did stall, I should immediately jam the throttle to full power and tilt the nose up only as I gained speed. Hopefully I would still have enough altitude to do a stall recovery.

I practiced stalls and stall recoveries over and over until recoveries became second nature. To set things up, I would first put the plane into a slow descending approach to an imaginary runway, then pull up continuously on the yolk, tipping the nose higher and higher until a stall occurred. The stall event is pretty dramatic, with the nose of the plane dropping down precipitously and aiming toward the ground. This feeling reminded me of some scary carnival rides I experienced as a kid. I became quite proficient at rapidly applying full power and then raising the nose of the plane away from the ground. Of course, this practice was typically done at three thousand feet, not at three hundred feet on my way to an actual landing.

When I sensed my first marriage wasn't working, my initial actions were similar to pulling the nose of the plane up. I argued with and scolded my wife and wouldn't listen to my parents, who offered sound advice. I began going out at night and returning late or not at all. When I noticed the pending stall and tried to recover, it was too late. I stalled and hit bottom with a divorce.

Perhaps I learned something from this crash landing. Some years later as a new manager, I was confronted with a difficult employee. This was my first encounter with an aggressive, unreasonable employee under my management. My initial reaction was to try to avoid this person. I canceled meetings, looked the other way, and generally delayed the inevitable confrontation. When confrontation did occur, I tried to use common sense and a friendly approach to our differences of opinion. To my surprise, this only made things worse. In looking back, my behavior was clearly the equivalent of pulling the nose of the plane up. And in fact, I was just about to stall in handling this situation when this employee went behind my back to complain to the Human Resources Department. My experienced supervisor quickly arranged some urgent counseling for me, and after a few weeks I was better equipped to manage this person successfully. With the help of this supervisor, I made a recovery from what was surely a pending stall that might have cost me my job.

I valued the ability to make stall recoveries in my plane and now in my life. The recognition that I may not reach the runway is the first step. And I know that quick and effective action, rather than mishandling or avoiding the problem, is essential.

Fear, Anger, and Control

It was late summer of 2008, and my instructor and I were flying back from an all-afternoon lesson. By now, dusk was setting in. I was at the controls and feeling some fatigue. Even though we agreed that I was close to being ready for my FAA private pilot's test, this particular lesson had not gone all that well. Our home airport was Palo Alto, a single runway airport, and my instructor wanted to make sure that I was comfortable landing and taking off from airports other than our home base. We had flown out to Concord Airport, which has a complex set of runways. I became uneasy about communicating with the tower and following the controller's instructions for which runway we were assigned for landing. My instructor tried to calm me down, and I finally brought the plane in for an okay landing. After takeoff, a lingering anxiety remained. I wouldn't call it fear—yet. On the way back to Palo Alto, we needed to pass near to Livermore Airport, a busy airport with two runways. It was getting dark, but my instructor told me to do a landing at Livermore. Fear struck. Suddenly, I forgot the wind direction, the radio frequency for Livermore tower, and the runway numbers there. I drew a blank. "My controls," my instructor said when she sensed I had frozen.

Upon landing at Palo Alto, I apologized and said that I didn't know what happened. "Don't worry about it; this is not unusual," she told me. My instructor and I agreed that the FAA test flight needed to be put off for a while.

This episode was unusual for me, and it bothered me a lot.

I woke the next day angry. After months of work, it seemed that I was nowhere near where I thought I was. I began to rationalize that I had been setup to fail by my instructor. She should have known how tired I was. I headed out to the Palo Alto Airport in a negative frame of mind.

All pilots have personal limits on how much wind is considered safe for them to fly. The wind that day was strong. In fact, the wind velocity was close to my personal limit for safe flying, with some gusts well above my limit. Furthermore, the wind was blowing sideways across the runway rather than in the more pilot-friendly headwind direction. This is known as a cross-wind and presents challenges even for experienced pilots. While I didn't have my license yet, I was approved to take the plane out by myself as long as I didn't bring any passengers along. I knew the wind was strong, but my head was spinning with anger, and I wanted to work out my aggression in the plane. I cannot think back on this dumb behavior without shaking my head. I have to say, there appear to be dark recesses in my mind that I hope I will rarely if ever again need to explore.

By now you know that this story doesn't have a good ending; and it shouldn't. After a short flight, I was determined to demonstrate that my landings could be excellent, even in strong winds. I would show the world that I was coming along nicely as a pilot. On my first approach to the runway, I was blown so far off course by the crosswind that I was not even over pavement. Before touching the ground, I shoved in the throttle to full power, tipped the nose up and aborted my landing attempt. I flew back around the airport traffic pattern, and the controller in the tower cleared me for another landing attempt. By now, I'm sure that he was watching me carefully. I did get the plane on the ground this time, but instead of landing correctly on the two main wheels, I hit the runway with the delicate nose wheel first, then wheel-barrowed along for a distance. Finally, the two main wheels touched pavement, I applied brakes and got off the runway. "Whew, glad my instructor wasn't with me," I said to myself.

I tied the plane down in its assigned parking place, snuck out to my car, and headed for home.

About an hour later, my phone rang. "Were you flying today?" my instructor asked.

During my initial training, I was not aware of how fear and anger might express themselves in my flying. I was shocked by these two incidents, and in looking back, I realize that I didn't, and maybe still don't, completely know myself. I refer to these incidents as operational blackouts.

Fear and anger have the power to cloud a person's mind. The antidote is control. In flying, I learned that it is essential to maintain control at all times. For me, the formula for gaining control is first excellent training, then practice and experience, all leading to confidence. The instant that fear or anger dominate, you are done with flying.

These are lessons that may be easier said than done in nonflying situations. I remember becoming frozen with fear when I lost sight of my eight-year-old son in the surf along a beach in Hawaii. But I quickly gained control, ran to the edge of the water, located him, and directed the lifeguard to save him. Another time, when I found out that one of my fellow workers had reported false disparaging stories about my management style to our Human Relations Department, I recall feeling a flash of anger. But I put the anger aside promptly and went through the necessary steps to correct this unpleasant situation. Fear and anger continue to push their way into my life from time to time, and remembering the flying episodes has assisted me in maintaining control.

The Radio

Right from the start, I didn't enjoy radio communication. The controllers seemed to pride themselves on how fast they could talk. They also used a jargon that you better learn or you will soon be over your head. As soon as I realized that I could avoid all but the most essential radio communications, I took that course of action. When my choice for routing between point A and point B was between flying in controlled airspace in radio contact with a controller versus uncontrolled airspace with no radio contact required, I inevitably chose the latter.

I still am not positive whether I avoided elective radio communication due to insecurity or inexperience. I realize that these problems are interrelated, with my lack of confidence leading to avoidance, and avoidance resulting in lack of the practice that could build up my confidence.

I also realize that subtle and sometimes not-so-subtle factors influenced my aversion to radio communications. Only one month after receiving my private pilot's license, I decided to fly to Monterey Airport, land, and then takeoff and fly back. This turned out to be a complex assignment, since Monterey is Class C Airspace. Flying in Class C Airspace was new for me and required a complicated set of radio communications, both for incoming as well as for departing air traffic. I managed this pretty well flying in, but trouble cropped up on my departure. As I took off, I became confused about when to switch my radio frequency from the airport tower to the regional radar controller. I jumped the gun and switched too soon, confusing everyone. I dealt with the FAA regional office in San Jose for several weeks after that, finally being excused and told never to do this again.

I never broke this pattern over my seven years of flying. However, reflecting on my radio aversion and its origins has taught me a good bit about dealing with similar situations in real life. For example, I've never felt comfortable or confident with statistics and would like to avoid them in my professional life. But the more I avoid using statistics, the less practice and confidence I have with this essential skill set. In contrast to certain radio work in flying, statistics are not elective in my profession. I decided that rather than avoid, I must learn and use them. Keep an eye open for this situation in your own life. You usually can deal with it once you recognize what is going on. That is, if you chose to.

Close Calls

One fine sunny Sunday afternoon, my wife and I were out for a pleasant flight. We were approaching Petaluma Airport, which is nontowered. Pilots in the area are expected to tune in to a common radio frequency and advise one another of where they are, what they plan to do, and when they will do it. While this sounds chaotic, the system works well—99 percent of the time.

Ten minutes earlier I had announced my incoming position, and now I announced my intentions to land on runway 29. Suddenly, not more than twenty feet above me, another small plane flashed across my flight path, nearly causing a collision. In shock, my first reaction was that I was somehow out of position in the landing pattern. My radio then came alive with the voice of the pilot who nearly hit me. "Write down my phone number, and give me a call later in the day."

Shaken up, my wife and I landed and had lunch. I still wasn't sure what had happened when I called the pilot later. He apologized and said, "That was my fault. I was out of position and didn't see you. In fact, I was going the wrong way around the traffic pattern."

Rather than pat myself on the back that the close call wasn't my fault, I just felt numb from this frightening experience.

Another day, flying alone, just after takeoff I noted something wasn't right. As I tried to adjust the upward pitch of the plane to provide a safe takeoff trajectory, I realized that the trim wheel, a hand-operated control wheel used to fine-tune the position of the flap that determines the up or down pitch of the plane, was frozen in place. The wheel couldn't be moved, and my ability to operate the plane safely was in question. I called the tower and informed the controller of the situation. "Check to see if your autopilot has become inadvertently engaged," he suggested.

"No, it isn't," I told him. "I would like to circle around and try to land as soon as I can," I requested.

I wasn't sure how I was going to make the plane level off and allow for a descent to the runway. "I am holding all traffic in the area, and you are cleared for landing when able," the controller said.

Suddenly, I remembered the principle that at slower speed, your altitude is determined by your power, not your flaps. I reduced power and sure enough, even though I couldn't trim the flap to push the nose down, the plane slowed and began to descend. I lined up for the approach, controlling my descent entirely by power adjustments. Fortunately, the nose got down enough to allow me to land level with the runway. After a tense but safe landing, I advised maintenance of the problem; sure enough it was a mechanical failure and not of my doing. While I could take some solace that I did not cause this situation by mistaken flight preparation or control, I simply exhaled and was thankful to walk away from the landing.

I have had close calls in flying and in life. A near-serious accident and a personal crisis each leave residual effects. A near collision with a plane flying too close overhead and finding out that your wife has a new lump in her breast leave you feeling drained and helpless. I've found that exercising good judgment, good decision-making, and gaining as much experience and skill as possible will reduce the chance of a close call. Given enough time in the air, however, all pilots will experience one.

Joy

Life has taught me that it can be exhilarating to be different and to feel special. Remember, 99 percent of the public will never fly in a small plane, let alone pilot one. For me, it was a mind-altering experience. I saw things I could never see any other way. Flying in a conventional commercial airliner could not provide the views and freedom I experienced in a small plane. Have you ever wondered what is on top of that mountain, what the hills along the Pacific Coast are hiding, what it looks like to fly over that exclusive neighborhood, or what Napa Valley looks like from the air during the colorful fall harvest season? How about exploring the Golden Gate Bridge from the air, or flying down to Monterey and taking a tour of the famous golf courses … by air?

For those of you who have enjoyed listening to Ludwig van Beethoven's *Ninth Symphony*, the rapture evoked by the last movement will likely be captured as you fly among sights that few others will ever see. This movement is called "Ode to Joy," and features the orchestra, choir, and soloists singing their hearts out in joy. I would often hear the glorious strains of "Ode to Joy" as I flew through the sky.

And on the ground, a sense of gravitas lingers over the airport. Flying lessons and life lessons intermingle. The lasting impact of all this for me is respect and gratitude that I could be part of the aviation community, at least for a few years.

My Forty Years with Wine: The Early Years

Up until I was about twenty-eight years old, out of school and doing a residency in medicine in Boston, my alcoholic drinks were limited to beer and the occasional gin cocktail. Of course, I knew of wine and had sampled such classics as Blue Nun, Mateus, and Cold Duck. The sweetness alone was off-putting, but the smell was even worse.

"Would you like to come over to my place for dinner tonight?" my new girlfriend, Diane, asked one day.

This was someone I really hoped to get to know better. I certainly wanted to accept this invitation, and furthermore, make a good impression. What does a proper guest do at a nice dinner? Friends suggested that I bring a good bottle of wine. Fine, but I had a problem: I knew nothing about wine.

Knowing this wasn't rocket science, I headed to a well-regarded wine store in Boston. The salesperson asked my price range, and we settled on a red French Bordeaux wine called Château Lanessan. This château is regarded as a reliable red Bordeaux wine, but of course at the time, I didn't have a clue about these details. All I knew was that it was a bottle of red wine deemed by an expert to be good.

The wine was delicious and complemented the dinner prepared by my host, who also knew little about wine but clearly enjoyed it. I could make a long story short by simply telling you that I ended up studying, collecting, and drinking wine for the next forty-plus years. I also ended up marrying this new girlfriend, and we recently celebrated our forty-second wedding anniversary. However, the longer version of the story is worth telling.

Shortly after this seminal experience, I finished my residency in Boston and moved to the Washington, DC area, in order to do research at the National Institutes of Health in Bethesda, Maryland. Washington, DC, was, and still is, a great wine town with many fine shops and wine groups. The emphasis has always been on European wines rather than American. This tradition began in the eighteenth century with Thomas Jefferson, who was our ambassador to France before becoming president, during which time he imported many bottles of fine French wine to be enjoyed at his Monticello estate. His enduring comment on wine is, "Good wine is a necessity of life for me."

My newfound interest in wine flourished in DC. In those days, namely the early 1970s, for American oenophiles, there was French wine, and then there were all the others. The others didn't really count much. The bible was a book written by Alexis Lichine, a wine importer, called *Wines of France*. A wine merchant that I had befriended directed me to this book, and it was a key to my approach to wine. To this day, if a wine is not French, it is going to have to prove itself to me. If it is French, I relax and 99 percent of the time I am pleased.

So what is meant by *French*? At least in those days, French meant either Bordeaux or Burgundy. Areas like the Loire Valley, Rhone, and Alsace, for example, were not taken seriously. Champagne, being a special occasion wine, was taken seriously but rarely drunk. Also, for purposes of this discussion, Bordeaux and Burgundy wines are referring specifically to red wines. The white wines from these regions can be wonderful, but as one pundit stated, "The first responsibility of wine is to be red."

The Bordeaux wine region comprises 280,000 acres of vineyards, producing sixty million cases of wine annually. The region surrounds the city of Bordeaux, which is the worldwide wine industry capital, accounting for around $15 billion per year in wine trade. Bordeaux is located just inland from the Atlantic Coast, about three hundred miles southwest of Paris, along the river Garonne. The region is naturally divided into right bank and left bank areas by the Gironde estuary, with the majority famous wine-producing châteaux located on the gravel-rich left bank. Cabernet sauvignon is the predominant red grape used on the left bank, and merlot is predominant on the right bank.

While there are thousands of privately owned wine-growing estates in the Bordeaux region, my job to learn about the wines was simplified by several facts. First of all, while the area is large, there are only seven prime territories in which the famous wines are grown, and these areas are small in size. These collections of vineyards are located in communes or subregions, including: Saint-Estèphe, Pauillac, St. Julien, Margaux, and Graves on the left bank and Saint-Émilion and Pomerol on the right bank. Furthermore, within each of these seven areas, relatively few châteaux make famous wines. Everyone serious about wine is expected to memorize these particular châteaux, seek them out, and understand their taste characteristics.

A further guide for the wine student is the "Bordeaux Wine Classification of 1855." In honor of the 1855 Exposition Universelle de Paris, Emperor Napoleon III requested that a panel of experts classify the leading wines of Bordeaux, in order that they might be displayed at the exposition in a meaningful manner. Judging criteria were primarily taste and commercial value. This government panel classified the great Bordeaux wines into what are known as First, Second, Third, Fourth, and Fifth Growths. Thus, the student of wine is guided efficiently toward the top wines of the Bordeaux region and is expected to memorize these wines according to their classification. The most famous of these wines are the First Growths, which include Châteaux Latour, Lafite, Margaux, Haut-Brion, and Mouton Rothschild. Remarkably, now some 160 years later, this classification holds up well and continues to drive commercial success.

New York is one of the top cities in the world for drinking fine Bordeaux, and Diane and I would frequently visit New York to dine at one of the many fine French restaurants of the day. One evening while dining at La Caravelle, a restaurant that prided itself on the depth of Bordeaux selection available, I was approached by the captain. "You two seem to know what you are doing when it comes to wine," he observed. "How would you like to gamble tonight?"

"Well, it depends," I responded. "What is the game?"

"We have an old bottle of Bordeaux in our cellar that has no label," he continued. "We found the bottle at the bottom of a bin and the label apparently dried out and fell off. We have no idea what is in the bottle. Of course, if we pull the cork, we will know, because all corks in bottles of Bordeaux wine are stamped with the name and year of the wine."

"So what's the proposition?" I asked.

"I would be prepared to sell it to you for drinking with your dinner for a modest price, which could be well under its value," he offered. "Of course, the gamble is that it may end up being overpriced for what you pay. We will only find out the winner once the cork is pulled."

After a short chat with Diane, who seemed eager to play the game, I said, "Okay, what is the modest price?"

"Fifty dollars," he offered.

In those days, around 1973, fifty dollars was on the high side for most restaurant wines. But, knowing the standards at La Caravelle, I felt that my chances for a good wine were reasonable.

"Okay, let's do it," I mumbled.

The captain quickly disappeared, and within ten minutes he brought the bare bottle to the table. I inspected it carefully, noting that it was covered with dust. The level of wine inside reached the shoulder of the bottle when I stood it up, indicating that the cork was sound and had not been leaking wine or letting too much air inside the bottle. All of this was reassuring.

The ceremony began. Opening an old bottle of wine is a tricky business, best handled by an experienced operator. The captain carefully twisted and guarded the cork as he pulled it out. Intact! Then—the moment of truth. The cork was passed to me for inspection—1961 Château Latour. Ladies and gentlemen, we have a winner. This was a First Growth wine from one of the outstanding years of the twentieth century. I guessed, and later confirmed, that the fair market value of this wine was five hundred dollars, not fifty. Today, this wine sells for five thousand dollars. And the wine was superb, offering an unctuous display of fresh berry flavors with an underlying hint of chocolate and mint.

A few years later, I was asked by a pharmaceutical company to tour several Swiss cities and provide lectures on antibiotics. At the end of a long, hard week, I finished the tour in Zurich. The company representative made arrangements to meet me at my hotel, where he kindly invited me to celebrate our successful tour with dinner at a venerable and well-regarded restaurant. After we sat down, my host leaned over with a smile on his face. "We have arranged with management here for a special treat," he said, appearing excited at the prospect.

"What pray tell have you arranged?" I said in a slightly tired voice.

"The manager has given permission for you to go down to their wine cellar and select any bottle of your choice to have with our dinner," he effused.

This caught my attention, and as tired as I was, I couldn't refuse. "What are the rules?" I asked.

"Very simple; you have five minutes to find a wine, and it can be any wine in the cellar," he explained. "It can be from any vintage and can be from any region. The value of the wine is not a restriction."

I was now excited. The manager suddenly appeared with a smile on his face and beckoned me to follow him to the cellar. He was holding a large watch and clearly was going to enforce the five-minute rule.

"Okay, here we are," he said as we descended the poorly lighted stairway. "I am going to open the door and start timing you. When five minutes is up, I will call out for you."

He opened the door to the wine cellar, and my eyes beheld a dazzling display of filled-to-the brim wine racks stretching far into the distant corners of the room. The cellar was well-lighted, and I knew my first task was to figure out how things were organized. After a couple of precious minutes, it was clear that the cellar was partitioned by wine regions, such as Bordeaux, Burgundy, Rhone, and other French areas. Non-French wines were located farther away, which didn't bother me as I was only interested in French wines. The closest section was Bordeaux and this was set up next to the Burgundy section. How convenient—I had my plan.

I reasoned that Bordeaux wines would be more predictable than Burgundy, as they are noted for consistency. Also, as I knew the great vintage years for Bordeaux, my plan was to concentrate on this section of the cellar. The greatest years in the twentieth century were 1927, 1945, and 1961. I hoped to spy a classified Bordeaux from one of these years. Time was passing, and I needed to get going. I couldn't locate any wines from 1927 or 1945, but there were plenty from 1961. Even by narrowing to 1961 Bordeaux, my job was still difficult. Virtually all the great châteaux were present in the bins, and all the bottles I examined looked to be in perfect condition. I made that judgment by checking the level of wine in the bottle to make sure it was not too low. The fills were all great, well above the shoulder of the bottle. There was no reason to expect that air had leaked in or that wine had evaporated out. This is the reward for being located only a few hundred miles from the châteaux with only short distances for the wine to travel and minimal chance for damage to the bottles.

One minute left, and I needed to choose. I selected a 1961 Château Léoville-Las Cases. This is a Second Growth wine from St. Julian and is regarded to be on a par with the First Growths in quality. I had never had the opportunity to taste it, and now I would. The manger appeared promptly at the five-minute deadline and showed me up the stairs to my table. He carried the bottle for me and gave it the reverence it deserved.

Settling back into my seat at table, my companion was clearly impressed. Remember, he was also going to reap the rewards of the wonderful adventure. The wine was delicious, filled with nuances of plums and soft burnishes of wood. The dinner was pretty darn good too, featuring seared foie gras, lobster soufflé, and a wonderful duck breast that was pan seared and flamed with an orange liquor at the tableside. I was in heaven.

As a student of wine, my job was to learn about a relatively small number of Bordeaux wines. Burgundy wines were another matter. Other than both being alcohol-containing beverages made from grapes, there are few similarities between the Bordeaux and Burgundy wines and the systems used in their respective regions.

The Burgundy wine region consists of a long, narrow band of wine-growing villages located about three hundred miles east of Bordeaux and two hundred miles southeast of Paris. The region does not have large estates with beautiful chateaux producing large crops of grapes as is so commonly seen in Bordeaux. Rather, hundreds of individual wine growers own small parcels of land and produce small crops of grapes each year. To give an example, Chateau Latour, one of the most famous of all the Bordeaux wines, produces about eighteen thousand cases a year. Romanée-Conti, the most famous wine produced in Burgundy, produces about four hundred cases a year.

Burgundy wine growers may use their grapes to make their own wine and sell it under their domain name; or they may sell their grapes to large companies that pool the fruit from many growers into larger production and sell the wines under their brand name. These companies are called negociants; Louis Latour, Louis Jadot, Bouchard Père et Fils, and Joseph Drouhin are among the most famous.

As in Bordeaux, the best wines in Burgundy are made in a small segment of the total area. This prime growing area is called the Côte d'Or, which begins in the north at the city of Dijon and ends about twenty-five miles to the south in the village of Maranges. The wine-growing land along this corridor is only about two miles wide. In contrast to Bordeaux, the wines of Burgundy do not have a long-standing hierarchical classification system. However, Burgundy wines are classified by the government according to their quality, with a Grand Cru designation for the best wines, followed by premier cru, and then wines designated only by their villages or regions.

Burgundy wine tastes different from Bordeaux wine. This makes sense since the grape used to make Burgundy, the pinot noir, is quite different from the grapes used for Bordeaux. Bordeaux is usually a blend of Cabernet Sauvignon, Merlot, Cabernet Franc, and Petit Verdot. In contrast, Burgundy is not a blended wine. The complexity of Burgundy wine taste is dictated by *terrior* rather than blending. The concept of terrior, which means taste of the soil, is that various parcels of land have subtle differences in chemical and physical composition, and this influences and results in a distinctive flavor unique to that parcel. Wines grown within a few miles of one another may express distinctly different terroir-driven flavors. As an example, one of the most famous vineyards in Burgundy is called La Tâche. This plot of land is only fifteen acres in size, yet is known to produce wines with a taste unique and different than any other wine made in Burgundy. I read about the oriental spice and incense typical of La Tâche and set out to put this to the test. Sure enough, as I sipped a glass of La Tâche for the first time, I was immediately aware of these oriental flavors. Furthermore, no other Burgundy wines that I tasted before or since displayed this unique terroir. The wine student is expected to learn how to distinguish between these vineyards based on these tastes. This is a unique and difficult aspect of learning Burgundy wine.

But perhaps most difficult about Burgundy is the unpredictability of wines even from the same village and same year of harvest—known as vintage. In Bordeaux, uniformity across the commune and vintage is the norm. In Burgundy, the quality of the wine and style of taste is totally at the discretion of the individual winemaker. Since there are hundreds of different winemakers, each with their own vision of wine and each with their own quality standards, this makes learning about the wines of Burgundy considerably more difficult.

Some generalizations are possible; wines made in the north, known as the Côte de Nuits, tend to be richer and heavier than wines made in the south, known as the Côte de Beaune. Also of no surprise is that Grand Cru wines often, but not always, taste better than Premier Cru wines. This is usually, but not always, reflected in the price. Wines made in a harvest year deemed by the experts as a good year are usually, but not always, better than wines made in an off year. A widely known fact is that a wine from a good producer in a so-called bad year may be better than a wine from a lesser producer in a good year. If you are beginning to wonder if the only way to be sure of the quality of a given Burgundy wine in a given year is to taste it, you are correct.

To use a metaphor, Bordeaux wines are elegant and formal people, behaving properly in businesslike fashion—tuxedoed gentlemen with long-gowned women at their sides. In contrast, Burgundy wines are movie stars, wearing sunglasses and sporty outfits, driving their racy cars. In Burgundy, the staid, perfectly manicured chateaux of Bordeaux are nowhere to be seen. When Diane and I first visited Burgundy in 1978, we were impressed with the beauty and ruggedness of the area. Dirt roads wound through rolling hills and between small plots of vines. You could park your car by the most famous Burgundy vineyards, such as Le Montrachet, La Tâche, and Richebourg, get out, and collect rocks as souvenirs. I still have my collection in my wine cellar.

Diane and I wisely met with some local merchants in Boston before our trip, asking them to set up personal visits for us with winemakers with whom they did business. This was a critical move, as drop-in visits for wine tastings are unheard of in Burgundy except at the mass-production companies. We had appointments with several small and well-regarded vintners, and the visits were impressive. One memorable stop was in the Gevrey-Chambertin village, located in the northernmost part of Côte De Nuits. The vineyard, called Mazis-Chambertin, is one of the Grand Crus and is highly sought out. The winemaker, named Maume, was cordial, and with our letter of introduction, we were ushered to the cellar. There we were offered tastes of recently made wine, which was still fermenting in wooden casks. I found it hard as a nonwinemaker to taste and predict the end product, but it was fun to try. A few years later, I saw this same wine selling in the United States for about two hundred and fifty dollars a bottle.

Our last visit in the morning was with a jolly, red-faced vintner who unexpectedly invited us to join him for lunch. My spoken French was not good, but it was sufficient to conduct some basic conversation. We accepted.

No one had warned us about the gargantuan appetites and drinking capacity of Burgundians. The concept of a light lunch on the run, we later learned, was nonexistent in Burgundy. We blissfully followed our host down the road in our rental car, hoping for a pleasant and quick lunch after which we could be on our way. We had a full afternoon planned, including visits to several important winemakers' cellars. Also, if time permitted, we hoped to stop in the village of Beaune, where we would visit the famous Hospices de Beaune, a charitable hospital funded by an annual wine auction.

The restaurant for our lunch was in a charming stucco farmhouse surrounded by short rows of vines. A few animals wandered around here and there, and we were greeted by a large, overly friendly golden retriever. Our host and the proprietor were clearly old friends, and no menus were needed.

Within minutes, a waiter placed a large carafe of basic red Burgundy wine on the table and filled our glasses to the brim. *"A votre santé,"* exclaimed our host as we all clinked our soon-to-be-empty glasses.

A huge steaming plate of escargots, redolent with garlic, suddenly landed on the table. Baskets of still warm, crusty loaves of French bread were already waiting for us. The gusto with which our host dug in spurred Diane and me to eat heartily as well. In less than five minutes, our jolly group had cleaned the platter. Upon finishing our generous lunch, I wondered if dessert would be served, or maybe we would just finish lunch with coffee. The original carafe of wine was long gone, replaced by another full one.

Suddenly, the unexpected happened. A rotund and sweating waitress brought a big bowl of steaming ham hocks to the table. "These are typical of Burgundy meals, served almost every day," our host happily explained. "I hope that you enjoy pork and be sure to try the mustard."

Have you ever been at a meal where the host is obviously enjoying everything and able to eat copiously, while it becomes increasingly difficult for you to eat anything more? This was the situation, and I noticed a distressed look on Diane's face.

"To celebrate your visit, I brought along something special for lunch," our host said proudly.

He reached into a canvas bag under the table and pulled out a bottle of his very own wine. The bottle was a Chambertin Grand Cru and was by my estimate worth over one hundred dollars on the retail market. Chambertin is one of the most highly regarded of red Burgundy wines, and after two carafes of ordinary red wine, I was interested to taste something special. But did I have the capacity?

Simultaneously, a big platter of hot potato salad with all the trimmings arrived. The trimmings were bowls of onions, pickles, olives, and, of course, several kinds of mustard. Three just-baked baguettes of crispy bread were also proudly presented to us. Now we had the proper food to accompany the Chambertin.

After a taste of this very good wine, Diane said, "Could you excuse me for a few minutes?"

"Mai oui, madame," our host said in a reassuring fashion.

Diane did not return to the table that afternoon.

I was able to hold on for the entire two-hour lunch and even choked down some coffee at the end. I thanked our host profusely, and he said he needed to hurry back to his winery for a full afternoon of work. "Au revoir," he exclaimed as he drove out of sight.

I found Diane on the backseat of our rental car, curled up into the fetal position. I poked her, but no response. Upon returning to our hotel, I ask the desk clerk to cancel our dinner reservation for that evening at the local three-star Michelin restaurant. Best-laid plans …

Since I enjoy studying and memorizing, all of this information about Bordeaux and Burgundy came easily to me. Shortly after moving to DC, I began to apply my expanding knowledge of wine. I developed a routine that I called Saturday Rounds. Each Saturday afternoon, I headed out in my car to visit my favorite wine shops. In those days, McArthur Liquor, Plain Old Pearson, Calvert-Woodley, and Central Liquor were the shops that I frequented. I was well-acquainted with an individual in each shop and would deal exclusively with that person from week to week. My favorite shopkeeper was a man named Addy Bassin, the owner of McArthur Liquor. Addy enjoyed working the floor and getting to know his best customers. Sometimes he and I would debate the purchase of a particularly expensive wine. He called these rare and expensive wines "me-and-thee wines."

I knew the basics and could not be sold a wine from a bad vintage. However, since many of the wines I wanted to buy were young and candidates for aging in the cellar rather than immediate drinking, I needed to rely upon the knowledge of the salespeople, supplemented by reading recent articles and wine newsletters. A weekly haul would usually be about three to four cases. Most often, I would place these cases in my cellar and store them for future drinking.

Of course, tasting is critical to expanding one's wine knowledge, and associating specific tastes with specific wines and specific vintages is mandatory for a serious student of wine. While drinking a bottle at home is useful for learning, a far more efficient system is to open several bottles side by side and compare their tastes. This is best done in a wine group.

"Seeking interested and serous wine drinkers to join a tasting group," read the classified ad in the wine magazine. I called the phone number and reached Mike. "I am organizing a private group of people who are interested in learning more about wine," he explained. "The plan will be to meet frequently, perhaps weekly, and to drink several bottles based upon a theme at each meeting," he continued.

This plan seemed to fit my budding wine interest perfectly. "I would love to join your group," I said.

Our group consisted of five couples, the organizers Mike and Barbara, Neil and Winnie, Bob and Mimi, Jim and Liz, plus Diane and me. Our plan was to be detailed and thorough—just what I hoped for. We would spend an entire session on just one commune in Bordeaux or just one village in Burgundy. We soon began to learn the differences in taste among wines from these geographic areas. Furthermore, we began to understand the different tastes and appearance of old versus young wine. We learned that older wines have a rust-colored edge in the glass, while young wines have a deep red or even purple edge. We learned the taste of highly tannic wines, with their dry, woody finish, versus fruity wine, fully mature and soft on the palate. This training has held me in good stead for the rest of my life. To this day, I can taste a wine while blinded and guess or come close to guessing the identity of the wine.

As with all groups of diverse backgrounds, there were quirks to deal with in our wine club. One of the members would show up for our sessions wearing heavy perfume. I'm sure this was a long-standing routine for her. Unfortunately, the sense of smell, along with appearance and taste, is critical to evaluating fine wine. Some gentle hints didn't work, and finally Mike just asked her to stop showing up with the perfume. I think her feelings were hurt, but she stopped showing up with the perfume.

A more serious problem that cropped up was that Mimi seemed to want to sit on my lap. Toward the end of our sessions, she would say, "Jimmy, Jimmy, McBimmy, can I sit on your lap?"

Without waiting for an answer, she would then leap across the room, landing on my lap. This caused some serious heartburn for Diane. Surprisingly, Mimi's husband, Bob, didn't seem to mind at all. I received many postevent requests from Diane to block Mimi in her advances. My retorts that she meant no harm fell on deaf ears. Finally, I told Mimi that she couldn't sit on my lap anymore. She seemed quite disappointed.

A more formal and less quirky wine appreciation group was Les Amis de Vin. I came across this group by reading an article about wine appreciation groups in the *Washington Post*. This was a semicommercial group headed by an Italian man named Alfio. The group held wine-oriented dinners around town, during which members could be exposed to a wide variety of wine. Alfio also held some private lunches in honor of visiting wine experts. On one occasion, Diane and I were invited to his apartment for lunch and to meet one of the best-known wine critics of the day. Harry Waugh was English, and I had read his commentary in numerous wine journals. He was charming and engaging. I asked him whether he had he ever confused Bordeaux and Burgundy wine. "Not since lunch," he replied.

Finally, my three years in DC were done, and it was time to move back to Boston to begin work at Harvard Medical School. By now, my wine collection had grown to eighty-four cases, and moving this in the hot summer weather was of some concern. I seized upon a plan. I would hire some able-bodied men to help me load up a U-Haul truck. Then I would drive the truck to Boston overnight, when the temperature was cool. I prearranged for another crew of hired hands to meet me in Boston the next morning and load the wine into my cellar before the heat of day. The plan worked like a charm. To my knowledge, not a single bottle was damaged by this move.

The next eleven years were filled with great professional progress and also an expansion of my wine knowledge. In 1986, I accepted a job offer in the Bay Area of California. This next period of my life opened my eyes to many new wine regions, including California wines.

My Forty Years with Wine:
California, Here I Come

"What temperature do you want me to dial in, Doc?" said the driver of the large, refrigerated moving van.

"How about fifty-five degrees," I requested.

"Sure thing. See you in California," the driver nodded.

As the moving van pulled away from our house near Boston, I knew that my one thousand bottles of wine would be safe, despite the heat of summer.

It was August 1986; the family and I were headed west for my new job and what we knew would be a big change. Just how big was soon to become clear. As I settled into my seat on our plane ride to San Francisco, I wondered about many things. Among these was what the California wine scene would bring.

"Are you a wine snob?" my dinner host snarled.

"Not sure what you mean," I replied.

"Well, you seem to be turning up your nose at the wines I am serving tonight," he continued. "Aren't they good enough for you?"

I took a deep breath as I headed into a predictable debate. "I simply don't enjoy drinking Rombauer California chardonnay at 14.8 percent alcohol,"

I advised. "I also cannot deal with the Pahlmeyer California cabernet at 16 percent."

"What does alcohol percent have to do with this?" came the predictable reply.

"Where do I start?" I thought to myself. Then I got an idea. "Have you ever tried a European wine with alcohol at about 13 percent?"

"Aha, just as I thought; you are a snob and only want to drink European wines," my host challenged.

This particular conversation took place only a few weeks ago. However, it is similar to many encounters I have had since moving to California. In the early years, I was pleased to observe that California winemakers made every effort to mimic the European style of wine making. The grape stocks and blending formulas were direct imports from Europe, particularly France. The yeasts used in fermentation often were derived from European sources. Importantly, wines were usually balanced between fruit and acidity, with moderate alcohol levels being the norm. But then along came Robert Parker.

Robert Parker is among the most influential of all wine judges and wine writers. His monthly newsletter, *The Wine Advocate*, has gained a bulletproof reputation among many retail wine buyers, and he can influence the market success of any wine just in a few words and a tasting score of ninety or higher. As it turns out, Robert Parker loves big, dark, highly alcoholic red wines. *Voila*, the California winemakers are now making big, dark, highly alcoholic red wines.

Long before arriving in California, I knew that fermentation of grape juice using yeasts turns sugar into alcohol. The more sugar, and/or the longer the fermentation period, the higher the alcohol in the resulting wine. "We've had a lot of sunshine this growing season, thus more sugar in the grapes, thus higher alcohol levels in the wines," is something I frequently hear. And there is an element of truth to this in hot and sunny climates like California and Australia. But there is a simple solution to the overly sunny problem. Simply shorten the fermentation period and perform alcohol removal maneuvers. Instead, the sunny problem is more often an excuse for purposely producing and marketing wines with higher alcohol content, which are preferred by Robert Parker.

Why does alcohol content even matter? Well, it matters a lot, and for various reasons.

A few years ago, my wife and I were dining at the French Laundry restaurant in Napa Valley. The meal was just starting with some delicious eggs and caviar. "I need to go out to the parking lot and clear my head," I suddenly blurted out.

Something was hitting me like a sledgehammer, the room was spinning, and I had no idea what was going on. I had only had a few sips of wine, and wine had never done this to me. After I had been outside for about twenty minutes, the dizziness subsided and I went back to the table. The waiter had recommended a wine made by Turley Wine Cellars, which was made using zinfandel grapes. Upon examination of the label, I noticed that the listed alcohol content was 16.2 percent. To put this into perspective, the usual alcohol content for European wines is about 12.5 to 14 percent. I was on to something, and it wasn't good—at least not for me. After this experience, I watched as most of the winemakers in California began producing wines higher and higher in alcohol content.

Why was this going on? Certainly, this trend was not aimed at supporting better health or safer driving. While the threshold varies from person to person, my experience tells me that wines above 14 percent alcohol leave me in bad shape. Also, producing high-alcohol wines was not providing food-friendly wines. The taste of these uberalcoholic wines is actually hot in the mouth, and often smothers the balance of fruit and acidity. To be clear, these wines do not pair well with food. However, what these wines can do is stand out in critical wine tastings where the judges taste and spit. The juices used to make the wines are vigorously extracted from grapes, dark in color, and produce wines that are striking upon first taste. This striking first taste is what is used by Parker to assign his score.

I've tried arguing with confirmed California wine fans that highly alcoholic wines are not balanced. I've tried telling California winemakers they are no longer making food-friendly wines. I've tried to get them to admit that Parker and his marketing clout has ruined the style of modern California wines. I have had no luck. In fact, a number of my California wine-drinking friends have told me that they find the European wines too light and acidic, and they cannot get a good buzz on from these thin-style wines.

I'm happy to say in the last five or six years, San Francisco restaurants have moved away from these overly extracted alcoholic California wines and back to the classic, food-friendly European wines. Every single sommelier with whom I have discussed this issue—and I make it a point to discuss this issue all the time—agrees that the high-alcohol style is a mistake. These sommeliers keep a few token California wines on their wine list for those who insist, but they now have the courage to recommend the classic European wines that accompany their food so well.

When I first arrived in California, the concept of reserve bottles was well-known. For example, the venerable winery Beaulieu produced their regular Napa Cabernet Sauvignon, which sold for around six dollars a bottle. But they also made a reserve cabernet from their best vineyards called BV George de Latour Private Reserve. This was wonderful wine, made in classic Bordeaux style, and sold for the astonishing price of fifteen dollars a bottle. Reserve California bottlings were not well-known outside California in those days. Just before I left the East Coast, one of the wine merchants begged me to take some 1968 BV Private Reserve off his hands, which had been gathering dust, for a discounted price of six dollars a bottle. I took all I could.

Other vineyards produced reserve bottlings, including Robert Mondavi, Inglenook, Behringer, Joseph Heitz, and others. These were all more or less classic vineyards, and the price of the reserve bottles was modest by any standards. For most, it was easy to find bottles for under twenty dollars in those days. The exception was Heitz Martha's Vineyard Cabernet, which sold for the astonishing price of thirty dollars or more!

But trouble was brewing. In the late 1980s and early 1990s, a new breed of reserve cabernet bottlings began to appear. Phelps Insignia, Stags Leap Cask 23, Grace Family, and others were now being hyped by the wine critics as advanced styles and worth the price. The price had escalated to about fifty dollars per bottle. Naturally, the old guard did not want to be left out, and I suddenly noted with horror that BV Private Reserve and Robert Mondavi Private Reserve prices had jumped to fifty dollars per bottle. Of course, the taste was exactly the same as before.

Then it happened: In the mid-1990s, a phenomenon known as cult wines appeared. Harlan, Screaming Eagle, Colgin, Araujo, and other cabernets were introduced at prices that rose to over one hundred dollars per bottle. The justification for this unprecedented price for California wine seemed to be exclusivity and quality. Having tasted some of these wines, I admit that if you like the California style, they are as good as I have tasted. The wines are lush, jammy, and dark in color. They are made for early consumption, with no real objective to have them laid down in the cellar for long-term aging. Meanwhile, the classic vineyards, like BV, have fortunately called uncle and conceded the cult space. They continue to make wines of more classic style. And, if anything, the prices of the classic reserve bottlings seem to have moderated a bit.

Where will it stop? Some of these cult wines are now being released at retail for up to eight hundred dollars per bottle. At a recent auction, a bottle of 2012 Screaming Eagle sold for over two thousand dollars. And so a mission that began with the objective of pushing the hedonistic limits of California cabernet-based wines with attendant price increases has become the purview of investors and speculators. The public is relegated to simply reading about what is going on in this world of exotic cult wines and wondering if this was the intended mission.

Despite my battles with the chauvinistic California wine lovers, I came upon a group of like minded wine lovers with whom I could share fine wine and food together. I consider these people my wine family, or mafia of sorts. How the group was assembled might be interesting to others confronting the trials and tribulations of living in a California wine culture where unbalanced, expensive, and highly alcoholic wines are revered.

"You're a nice-looking young couple," my wife exclaimed.

We had only been in California for about a month and were desperate for wine-oriented experiences. This dinner was organized by a group called the American Food and Wine Society and was being held in a hotel ballroom, with the late Robert Mondavi and Julia Child the guest speakers. The nice-looking couple was seated alone at a small table near our large ten-person table. By now, those at our table had either departed or gone to sleep.

"Well, thanks, can we join you?" the nice woman replied.

Teri and Andy were in the process of deciding whether to keep living in New York, where they had a brownstone in Manhattan, or San Francisco, where they had just purchased a *pied de terre* in Pacific Heights. It didn't take long to bond with them over our mutual interests, particularly food and wine.

"Have you been to Chez Panisse yet?" Andy asked.

"No, is it good?" I replied.

"Well, I will make you an offer: if you try it and don't like it, I will pay for your meal."

We went together a week later, and Andy did not have to pay for our meal. During our dinner the discussion confirmed our mutual interest in fine wine and our shared East Coast sensibility in preference for European wines.

Couple one, done.

"Tennis Lessons, Call Jon" read the sign affixed to a signpost in my neighborhood. I called Jon, who said he was on his college tennis team, and now that he was home for the summer, he hoped to make a little money giving lessons on his parents' backyard court. "I would love to brush up on my strokes; when can we start?" I said.

"Can you come by at two o'clock tomorrow, and we can spend an hour looking at your game?" Jon replied.

The next day, I was pleased to meet Jon, a tall and friendly young man, who was eager to help me improve. After about thirty minutes of productive work, I asked him about his family.

"Oh, my dad is into food and wine and keeps a huge file on places to dine all over the world," he replied. "Some people consider this boring, but it really keeps him busy."

"Interesting," I thought to myself. "I would enjoy chatting with him about this sometime," I said in passing.

About a month later, my wife and I attended a neighborhood party. Also attending were Jon's parents, Fred and Shelby. Fred and I connected immediately, and we decided it was not if but just when we would get together to pursue our passion.

About two months later, Diane and I organized a dinner party at our home and invited Andy and Teri as well as Fred and Shelby. As the conversation progressed, Fred asked Andy where he grew up.

"I was born and raised in Shaker Heights, Ohio," Andy replied.

"Well, so was I," said Fred. "What did your father do?"

"He was a physician," said Andy. "How about yours?"

As it turned out, Andy and Fred grew up two blocks from each other, and their fathers, both physicians, worked at the same hospital. They had never met before this evening.

Couple two, done.

About two weeks later, Andy and Teri invited Diane and me to their home for dinner, explaining that they had a couple that they wanted us to meet. Harry and his wife, Ann, were a delight. Harry, a dermatologist, was one of the nicest people that I have ever met. Harry and Ann clearly relished good food and wine and were just the kind of people we wanted to befriend.

Couple three, done.

And then there was Lowell. I had known Lowell for many years, having attended medical meetings with him and often dining together at fine restaurants around the world. Lowell had moved from Los Angeles to the Bay Area about a year prior to me and was also looking for new wine and food friends. One of the first wine-oriented dinners that Diane and I hosted included Lowell. As a gift, he brought a 1959 Grand Echezeaux, Domaine de la Romanée-Conti. Fair market value … about two hundred dollars in 1986.

Our group complete.

Over the next twenty-five years, our little family met on many happy occasions to enjoy fine food and wine. A typical example was a lunch we organized at the French Laundry, a restaurant in Napa Valley. We sat down at 12:30 p.m., and halfway through lunch the chef-owner, Thomas Keller, appeared at our table holding an entire goose liver (foie gras), wondering whether we would like this cooked and served as a supplement to our meal. You know what the answer was. As we were departing at about 5:00 p.m., we began passing diners arriving for the evening meal.

As mentioned before, in the early days, I considered any red wine that was not either Bordeaux or Burgundy lumped into a basket that I called Rest of the World or ROW. This mind-set was rarely, if ever, challenged during my time living on the East Coast. This concept was challenged daily after moving to California. In addition to a continual push to get me interested in the wines of California, there was a general acceptance among my friends and fellow wine drinkers of basically any wine if it was perceived to be a good wine. Well, we can argue what is a good wine, but we cannot argue that there is a vast world of ROW wines to consider.

Pushed by my friends and influenced by the more casual wine culture in the west, I cautiously opened my mind to these other world wines. My experience is typical of how most staid, old-time oenophiles begin to explore wines beyond Bordeaux and Burgundy. The first ROW wines that I approached were wines from the Rhone wine district. Rhone wine seemed safe. It is still French and is located just to the south of my beloved Burgundy wine region. The grapes used in Rhone, however, are quite different from the pinot noir grape used in Burgundy. Initially, I needed to learn new grape names, like grenache, syrah, and mourvedre. Also, I learned that which particular grape is used for making a specific Rhone wine is at the discretion of the winemaker. In other words, in Rhone nothing is predictable.

The Rhones are best known for a wine called Châteauneuf-du-Pape, named after a little town located in the southern part of the Rhone region. The wine and local area are historically important. In 1308, Pope Clement V relocated the papacy to Avignon, a town in this wine-growing area. Over the years spanning the Avignon papacy, the quality and interest in local wines increased. Nowadays, the distinctive name and the famous papal castle displayed on the label have made this wine far and away the best-known wine from Rhone. However, with one exception, it is not the best wine made in Rhone. That exception is Château Rayas, where the legendary Jacques Reynaud built a reputation for world-class syrah-based Châteauneuf-du-Pape wines. Upon his death, the reputation has been maintained by his nephew, Emmanuel.

More elegant wines from the Rhone wine region are made in the north. The Côte-Rôtie and the Hermitage areas are the most reliable of all Rhone wines for elegance and complexity with prices to match. Once at a private dinner, I served a well-aged Hermitage that was blinded to the group. This bottle was mixed in among several fine Burgundy wines. Everyone guessed the Hermitage to be a Burgundy, and a good one at that.

After Rhone, I began to dabble cautiously in Italian wines. In the early years, I scoffed at drinking wines from Italy. That was a mistake. Some of my friends were raving about a new style of Italian wine called Super

Tuscan. Learning that these wines, made in the Tuscany region from a blend of grapes, often include cabernet sauvignon and merlot, gave me comfort. After all, aren't these the classic grapes from my beloved Bordeaux region? I began to try some bottles. Wow, why had I taken so long to find the likes of Sassicaia, Solaia, Ornellaia, and Tignanello? I also had read that some wines from northern Italy called Barolo and Barbaresco, made from a grape called nebbiolo, were quite good. Tasting these great wines of the Piedmont region, made by Gaja, Conterno, and Giacosa, was a revelation. And my favorite discovery of all was Brunello di Montalcino, a wonderful wine made from sangiovese grapes grown in Montalcino, a small village high upon a hilltop in Tuscany. These wines have been made by great houses, such as Biondi-Santi, for most of the twentieth century. I had to confess, Italy was making serious wines with elegance and style to challenge the best, and I was late to the table.

My success with Italian wines led me into an even murkier area: Spanish wines. Here, I quickly discovered was a hot area in modern winemaking. Several young winemakers, among them Alvaro Palacios, Peter Sisseck, and their acolytes were standing the wine press on their collective ears. Making wines in long dormant wine-growing areas, such as Bierzo, and making wines in little-known areas, like Priorat, an area south of Barcelona, and producing superexpensive boutique wines, such as L'Ermita, Pingus and Finca Dofi, are examples of where this new breed was going. Alongside this excitement, I discovered a classic set of Spanish wines made for decades in the Rioja, an area in northern Spain. I learned that these elegant wines, made from the tempranillo grape, can age for decades, and that they are some of the great wine values in the world. And finally, there was Vega-Sicilia Unico, a wine made in the Ribera del Duero region from a blend of tempranillo, cabernet sauvignon and merlot grapes. A Spanish friend gave me a bottle of 1982 Vega, and when I tasted it, I was sure that I was drinking Château Latour. My friends and I drank this wine alongside the 1982 Mouton Rothschild, and it was the crowd favorite. No surprise, since Vega is considered to be on par with the great First Growths of Bordeaux. It also sells for equivalent prices, often exceeding four hundred dollars a bottle. That was an eye-opener.

And so it went for this old wine curmudgeon. A set of ROW wines was being opened up under the sunny skies of California. Ironically, to this day, I am still not sold on the notion that California wines have reached the level of the upper level European wines.

I know, I know, what about the Judgment of Paris? On May 24, 1976, Steven Spurrier, a British wine merchant, organized a wine tasting in Paris, comparing California cabernet sauvignon wines to French Bordeaux and California chardonnay wines to French white Burgundy, made from 100 percent chardonnay. Importantly, the judges tasted the wines blind, meaning they were masked to their identity. All nine judges were French and were wine experts. The results have been interpreted in many ways, but there is no question that the California wines did better than expected. However, some have gone further to say that the winner was a California cabernet, Stags Leap Cask 23 vineyard. In fact, among the nine judges, first place was awarded to a French Bordeaux seven times. In two of these cases, the top choice was a tie between a French and California wine.

What I glean from this famous tasting event is that at the very top echelon, California could make a pretty good wine in those days. The vintages of the California wines in this tasting spanned 1969 to 1973, and during this period, winemakers were doing their best to emulate the French style, with lower alcohol, well-balanced, and food-friendly wines being the goal. Today, finding this type of wine in California is hard or impossible.

I am, at heart, a competitive person. I like to be at the top of my class; I like to be the first to finish my project; I even like to win at sports, if I can. So when I became aware of blind tasting wine, it was a natural for me. Blind tasting wine is felt to eliminate the bias one may have, favorable or unfavorable, if the label is revealed ahead of tasting the wine. If one is hoping to judge the quality of the wine, determine how likable the wine is, and in some cases even try to demonstrate one's ability to guess what wine is in the bottle, then tasting blind is the accepted way to proceed. There is little doubt that if you see that the label is a Château Lafite prior to your tasting the wine, you might overlook any flaws more easily. In all likelihood, knowing that you are tasting a Château Lafite Rothschild will make the wine taste better.

Once I began to attend events with a blind-tasting format, I learned that there is a potential competition involved. Each taster takes notes and writes down or states their comments and guesses on what wine is being presented. Let's say a flight of wine includes ten different bottles, all from the same region. A true expert should be able to guess the grape, country of origin, and perhaps come close to the year produced, for about five to six of the ten wines. There is no question that each taster hopes to do better than the other tasters in the group. Results are generally compared at the end of the tasting, when the identities of the wines are revealed. This is known as the unblinding. Since tasters have to announce their guesses in advance of the unblinding, a scorecard for each taster is available.

"It is such a pleasure to have our close wine drinking friends together with us for dinner tonight," I announced at the beginning of a typical dinner party in our home. "Tonight, we will be serving the wines in a blinded format. I look forward to hearing your comments and your guesses on what the wines are."

A more informal but just as exciting format is a friendly dinner party where the host serves a series of wines, each concealed as to its identity. A spirited discussion takes place after each bottle is served. After about fifteen minutes, the host asks the guests to make comments and guess what the wine is. Again, there is a type of gamesmanship in play here, and it feels good to do a good job of guessing in front of your friends.

What are some of the tricks of the trade for wine-tasting gamesmanship? If the host makes no attempt to disguise the shape of the wine bottle, even though it is covered in paper or foil, then one can quickly tell if the bottle has straight sides (e.g., Bordeaux, Italian, California cabernet) or has a wider shape with sloping shoulder (e.g., Burgundy, California, or Oregon pinot noir). Another obvious clue is the shape of the wineglass used, since different shapes of glasses are used for Bordeaux versus Burgundy. This latter clue may be misleading, however, since some hosts don't make an effort to be a purist on wineglass shapes, or worse yet, purposely put wrong wines in glasses. Individualized clues for a given host come from knowing their preferences, e.g., don't like Chassagne Montrachet, or what they have served before, assuming they won't repeat, of course. Knowing the good versus less good vintages is helpful, assuming your host won't serve from a bad vintage. This can be risky for some hosts, who may not pay attention to good or bad vintage years.

I have devised my own algorithm for guessing a blinded wine. Keep in mind that if you guess the grape, the age, and the country of origin, or at least American versus European, you get an automatic A-. If you also guess the town or place of origin, you get an A. And if you nail the actual bottle, A+. Believe it or not, I have had more than one A+ during my years with wine.

Step One: Age. Color and nose are your best guides. By the way, aroma or smell of the wine in the glass is called nose in wine tasters' vocabulary. For older wines, you look for a rusty brick-red color, and for younger wines you look for deep purple or bright-red color. Very old wines turn light brown. These colors are best observed at the edge of the wine as it sits in the glass. The nose also can hint of age, with musty even funky aromas common in older wines and raw, grapey aromas in younger wines.

Step Two: Grape. To guess the grape, pay attention to the glass. A tall, straight-sided glass should suggest cabernet or Italian grapes. A rounded bowl is more likely to hint at pinot noir. This assumes of course that your host serves the wines properly. The aroma can also suggest the varietal (i.e., type of grape), but the older the wine, the less helpful the aroma. Remember Harry Waugh, the wine critic, once said that the last time he confused Burgundy with Bordeaux was at lunch.

Step Three: Country of Origin. Keep in mind that wine tasters commonly call wines from California, Oregon, and Washington State *new world*. Wines from Europe they refer to as '*old world*. To guess the country, first of all, know the bias of your host. It is less likely that I, or some of my friends, will serve non-European wines. If you are at a Napa Valey event, it is highly likely that you are drinking California wine. Naturally, the taste of the wine helps (i.e., hot alcoholic in the mouth suggests new world, particularly California, while more acidic tasting wines suggest old world). There is no question that there is a stereotype of wines from certain countries that wine experts can identify. A California cabernet usually is distinctive from a European cabernet-based wine. Refer to the alcohol discussion above for details. For the pinot noir grape, however, the better Oregon pinot noir-based wines are more difficult to distinguish from French Burgundies. The highly alcoholic California pinot noir-based wines, however, are much easier to pick out.

Step Four: The A+. To receive an A or A+ is difficult. To guess a specific village of origin requires experience with terroir, or the taste of the soil. You either have this experience or you don't. To guess a specific bottle requires even more taste memory and some luck. There are certain wines that I do not miss. There is a unique mint flavor in Heitz Martha's Vineyard cabernets. There is a cedar taste and smell that I find in Château Lynch-Bages. There is a wonderful cedar and eucalyptus character that I note when tasting Château Mouton Rothschild. Oriental incense is notable as I smell and taste La Tâche. Yes, there are some occasions that I achieve an A+.

As I have reached my seventh decade of life, some interesting and pleasant changes have occurred in my life with wine. For example, those Bordeaux wines that I cellared thirty or even forty years ago are finally ready to drink. That long time invested in their care is paying off. The English actually have a term for Bordeaux wines that have finally reached their maturity. These wines are called *clarets*. And happily, once your claret has reached its apex of drinking, it usually stays at this plateau for several years before it begins to gracefully thin out with too much age.

The issue of human-aging versus wine-aging came to me as a sudden realization about forty years ago, during a visit to my home state of Oregon. I had kept in touch over the years with my favorite philosophy professor from the University of Oregon, my alma mater. Henry and I shared wine stories that only fellow wine collectors could appreciate. Upon the occasion of my visit, he and his wife, Pat, invited Diane and me to dinner at their home. Finding their home wasn't easy, as they lived in an old wooden house hidden deep in the Oregon woods. The roads were unmarked, but we finally drove up to the house, which sat in a clearing surrounded by huge fir trees and many varieties of ferns and moss, wet with recent rain. It was dark and cold outside, but the house was warmly lit.

"How would you like to pay a visit to my wine cellar?" Henry asked shortly after we arrived.

I could tell that he was eager to show it off. "Of course, I was hoping that you would ask," I replied.

We descended through a trap door cut from the wooden floor in a dimly lit back hall. Immediately I could see that the cellar was only about three feet in height, and that standing up and walking around to inspect the cases and cases of wine on display would be impossible. "Grab one of the rolling trolleys on the floor, and we will scoot around," Henry quickly instructed.

Problem solved. We looked like car mechanics as we lay on the type of contraption commonly used by mechanics to roll under a car and inspect the underside. But it worked. Up one aisle and down another we went. I marveled at the collection, which featured Bordeaux wines from vintage years dating back to the 1940s. I didn't see anything current however.

"Great collection, Henry, but what about the latest hot vintage release, 1970?" I inquired.

"Oh, that is way too young for me to purchase, Jim," he replied.

"I don't understand what you mean," I pursued. "You don't want to skip a new great vintage, do you?"

"You do the math," he responded. "I am seventy years old now, and it will take at least thirty years for the 1970 to mature and be at its peak for drinking. Why in the world would I lay that vintage down now?"

It took some time for me, being only thirty years old at the time and having just purchased twelve cases of wine from that very year, to fully grasp what my old professor was saying. I did over time come to understand, and now that I have passed that same seventy-year-old landmark, I too have stopped collecting Bordeaux for my cellar.

I have noticed a few other changes as I reach my seventies. In younger days, I prided myself in knowing the subtle differences among vintages for wines from all parts of the world. This was particularly important for Bordeaux and German wines that come from more northern regions and have some truly bad years. Even for Burgundy, Rhone, and Italian wines, a bad vintage would crop up from time to time. Nowadays, I do not worry much about keeping up on vintage ratings. Other than for Bordeaux and German wines, almost every year is rated above ninety points regardless of region. Why need I fill my head with subtle rating differences if it really doesn't matter?

I also notice a new breed of oenophiles at our social gatherings dedicated to wine. I used to be the one standing up and offering comments and critique. Now I am just sitting back and enjoying the comments of the new experts with their colorful vocabulary. I do wonder how a wine can display "hints of chocolate, layers of apricot, and an underlying fabric of nettles scented with strawberries" all at the same time.

My years with wine will continue. I am still as passionate as ever about what makes a good wine. I enjoy being adept at finding the best price-value on a restaurant wine list, and of course, I still delight at guessing correctly a wine served blind at my friends' dinner parties. But my greatest joy continues to be sharing rare and special wines that I have nurtured for years in my wine cellar. These wines appear like magic when the time and the people are just right. I have already begun selecting special bottles to serve at my seventy-fifth and eightieth birthday dinners. It is a bit early to plan for the eighty-fifth.

Looking at the big picture, I acknowledge that wine plays a major role in my life. Simply calling wine a hobby is not doing justice. I have ego invested in wine. I am proud that hard work, time at study, memorization, and a sense of gravitas are hallmarks of my life with wine. In addition, wine has added a wonderful dimension to my lifestyle and has been a joy to share with my wife of forty-one years.

Living with a Serious Person

My wife and I were in the kitchen the other night preparing dinner, when she suddenly turned to me and asked, "Do you wash your hair anymore?"

This question seemed so preposterous that I laughed. My wife is actually known to pose spontaneous, personal, and unusual questions. But this question took the cake. Granted I am no longer young, but I expect to live a few more years. Also, while the quantity of my hair has diminished, there is still recognizable and washable hair on my head. How could she think it fathomable that I might live out my days never again washing my hair?

For a moment or two, I pondered whether she had actually asked a question. I learned in college philosophy class that in order for a question to be a question, there needs to be a possibility for both a yes and no answer. For example, "Is water wet?" isn't a real question, since only one response is possible. Without getting lost in linguistic theory, if you grant that what my wife asked is qualified as a true question, then technically it appears that a no answer to her question is possible. But a no answer would mean that I am not going to be washing my hair ever again.

This all goes by way of saying that I wasn't sure how to respond to my wife. Since she is not known for her sense of humor, I knew she wasn't kidding. And I knew she expected an answer. So I asked her why she asked.

"I noticed that the shampoo level in your bottle of special shampoo has been staying at the same level over a long period," she said.

I suddenly realized that she was on to something. She wasn't 100 percent right, since I do still wash my hair, but not as frequently as in the past, and sometimes I just rinse my hair. I immediately became a bit defensive.

I hedged, "I might be using your shampoo instead."

"Why would you do that?" she said.

"I take some showers at our condo in the city and sometimes wash my hair there," I added.

"What percentage of the time do you do that?" she asked.

I couldn't answer that. But I did admit that sometimes I just rinse my hair in water rather than lathering up with shampoo.

"I read about someone who went ten years only rinsing his hair in water, never touching shampoo," I told her.

"Gross," she said.

It seemed to me that there might be a bigger issue at hand. This seemingly preposterous question, which was clearly not preposterous to my wife, inevitably involves who we are as a couple and how we view life, both separately and together.

It is said that opposites attract. I'm known by the family as a jokester. I tend to do a lot of kidding around with my wife, children, and grandchildren. This means that my wife's seriousness and my playfulness are opposite responses. Is it time now for me to acknowledge this difference? Is this a wake-up call that I need to recognize? If so, what value would be added to our relationship if I had a more nuanced appreciation of how we each tick?

I have noticed that men respond with humor more often than do women. However, my wife takes this difference to a new level. I wouldn't say that she has no sense of humor. Instead it would be more accurate to label her a serious person. An important distinction is that while I can be serious when appropriate, my mind-set differs from a fundamentally serious person. She and I have talked a bit about this before. She told me the home where she grew up was not a place where humor played much of a role. Her father was killed in World War II, and she was raised by three women: her mother, her grandmother, and their live-in maid, Emily. She was sent away to an all girls' boarding school by age twelve.

I visited her home many times when we were dating and always found it to be a pleasant, quiet, and somewhat formal place. There was no kidding around and certainly no joke telling or robust laughing. This was a contrast from my own childhood, which was raucous and filled with laughs with my two brothers. I respect this difference in our upbringing and the kind of adult it formed and have tried hard over our years together to recognize and pay close attention to the needs of a serious person. I try to listen to what she has to say and not assume she means anything other than what she says or wants.

As a result of growing up with two brothers, I've developed a habit of joking. Yet, after forty-plus years, it is still hard for my wife to detect when I am kidding her. Her default is always to believe that I am being serious, which frequently leads to her being annoyed, or worse yet, mad. Nevertheless, I haven't changed my approach in all these years. I continue to this day to make off-the-wall comments, kid, and pull her leg. Just the other day, she suggested that I e-mail my daughter to congratulate her on her excellent performance review at work. "I know I should but don't think I will," I replied.

This flippant comment went over poorly. "You don't understand feelings and how important this is," my wife reprimanded me. "I just knew you would blow this off."

Thinking about this now, I realize my comment wasn't kidding or funny: it was mean-spirited. I had gone too far, probably reacting negatively to my wife's telling me what I should do.

A valuable lesson was learned.

I e-mailed congratulations to my daughter within the hour and copied my wife.

How is this kind of behavior constructive or destructive to my relationship with my wife? Do I annoy her unnecessarily? Does she feel disrespected by me? In addition to our different approaches to humor, I realize that I may well have other behaviors that are quite different and perhaps difficult for my wife. I reasoned that examining our disparate approaches to interacting with others might provide clues.

For example, I unilaterally decide what information she provides to me is trivial. This information might include a wedding date for some friends, or plans for the weekend, and is often imparted in casual conversation. The problem arises when my wife expects me to remember what has been discussed. If I try to excuse myself by saying my memory is going bad, it never works. Saying that I misunderstood seems to be even more inflammatory. I've learned to just confess and apologize for my inattention. A comment like "my bad" actually seems to help.

Another example of my troublesome behavior is my tendency not to read thoroughly incoming e-mails from my daughter. E-mails that start with "my new shoes" or "sister-in-law's closet" just don't get read. The problem is the hidden message. It turns out that some, but not many, of these e-mails contain important information buried in the text. I don't pick up announcements like "Caden has a sore throat," or "Emily fell in the lake." Inevitably, my wife will ask what I think about the news from my daughter, and I will be forced to reply that I didn't see the e-mail. I have tried many approaches to dealing with this situation. My most frequent reply is: "I confused that e-mail with the one that I already read."

My wife never buys this, and I eventually just have to confess. Again, "my bad" strangely seems to help.

The two examples just given and my wife's responses underline an important personality trait, which I believe is inherent to being a serious person. For a serious person, family and friends are paramount in life's hierarchy and deserve utmost attention and care. No conversation, e-mail, telephone call or any communication with family can ever be deemed trivial. Likewise, all friends need focused attention. No conversation between my wife and friends begin without her introductory question of "how is" ... and you can fill in the blank. It could be your mother, your sister, your son, or any loved one. She is particularly attentive to people who are ill or otherwise indisposed.

My wife has learned that I cannot be depended upon to remember these details, and she instinctively reminds me to follow her lead. I am getting better at this, but it clearly doesn't come naturally. I still tend to forget people's names, fail to look someone in the eye, and I often overlook inquiring about people's families. I now realize that while I do not behave in the same way as my wife, I can benefit from the lessons taught by a serious person.

It is also important for me to understand that I cannot change a serious person like my wife into something she does not perceive as true to her ambitions and desires. A serious person embraces what she is doing completely, never questioning. A serious person has the confidence that he or she is on the right path and will not be deterred.

On rare occasion, I have tried to suggest an alternative set of goals or what I would visualize as a more ambitious set of activities for my wife. For example, I have tried to use some of our friends as successful role models. "Nancy is president of Hadassah, Katherine is president of the Mediterranean-Pacific Horticultural Society, Kathy is CEO of our library," I note. "You're intelligent and energetic; wouldn't you like to contribute more? The chance for making a real contribution is slipping away from you."

"I do what I am comfortable with," she says, "I am happy and appreciated." She remains content with being captain of the women's 9-Hole golf group at the club and head of mailing invitations for the local symphony gala event.

Least I shortchange myself in this analysis, there is clear indication that my wife enjoys and learns from some of my antics, as well as my more serious moments. I notice that she sometimes quotes me on important as well as less important matters. She listens carefully when I bring up some nuance that she may have missed. As an easy example, look at the various nuances I developed around her question, "Do you wash your hair anymore?" Obviously, all she was looking for was a yes or no answer. Also, using my humor, I am sometimes able to help see more sides of an issue.

I asked her recently if she likes metaphysical and mysterious concepts. While she knows these are fascinating to me, she of course said no. It is noteworthy that while we were attending a baseball game recently, the PA announcer invited a young girl to come up to the booth and introduce the players using the PA system. They showed her in action on the large video screen at the stadium. She was about nine years old and was wearing a sparkly green Mardi Gras-type mask. "Why does she need to wear a mask?" my wife asked.

"Don't you like her mask?" I replied.

"I don't like masks, period," she stated.

When I asked her if she likes to use metaphors, she said, "Is that when you call something one thing and it really is something different?" I learned from her response that she is so literal that the most she can do is define metaphor, rather than use them.

This discussion helped me to understand that in addition to being a serious person, my wife is a literal person. I am not, but I can benefit from this understanding. When I listen to my wife or others with her characteristics, I hear the conversation in a literal, concrete way. I do not attempt to read between the lines or otherwise add nuance. This can be a valuable skill set for someone who is not used to being literal.

Net, net ... the pros far outweigh the cons of living with a serious person. When my wife tells me something, it is always truthful. I do not have to spend time deciphering between kidding or pulling my leg versus what is factual. This is in contrast to the attempts at humor that I sometimes spring on her. In the end, my wife behaves in a consistent and predictable way. This is immensely appreciated when life becomes complex or stressful, such as at times of illness, family problems, or even death.

My wife is not weird, she is wholesome. Is this boring, does it mean that she lacks color or interest? Not a bit. It means that she is uniformly trusted and loved by family and friends. I must confess that my wife believes that I have odd and weird tastes at times. I do not apologize for this and hope that it might broaden my wife's understanding of the scope of life. However, I am secure in the understanding that it will never alter her approach to life. That would never happen with a serious person.